Building Fiction

How to develop
plot and structure

Building Fiction

How to develop plot and structure

Jesse Lee Kercheval

STORY PRESS
CINCINNATI, OHIO

Building Fiction: How to Develop Plot and Structure. Copyright © 1997 by Jesse Lee Kercheval. Printed and bound in the United States of America. All rights reserved. No part of this book may be reproduced in any form or by any electronic or mechanical means including information storage and retrieval systems without permission in writing from the publisher, except by a reviewer, who may quote brief passages in a review. Published by Story Press, an imprint of F&W Publications, Inc., 1507 Dana Avenue, Cincinnati, Ohio 45207. (800) 289-0963. First edition.

Story Press Books are available from your local bookstore or direct from the publisher.

01   00   99   98   97   5   4   3   2   1

Library of Congress Cataloging-in-Publication Data

Kercheval, Jesse Lee.
    Building fiction : how to develop plot and structure / Jesse Lee Kercheval.—
1st ed.
        p.   cm.
    Includes index.
    ISBN 1-884910-28-9 (pbk. : alk. paper)
    1. Fiction—Technique. I. Title.
PN3353.K47   1997
808.3—dc21   97-12754
                                                                          CIP

Designed by Clare Finney

Permissions

"Worry," by Ron Wallace, reprinted with the permission of the author.
"Stone Belly Girl," by Jamie Granger, reprinted with the permission of the author.

For Dan

CONTENTS

INTRODUCTION

In college I signed up for a beginning creative writing class, sure the professor would ease us into the art of creating fiction. I had in mind the kind of approach taken in foreign language classes. We would learn to say hello, goodbye, and good morning the first week, take a few weeks more learning the days of the week, months of the year, and how to count to twenty. By the end of the semester, we would probably have worked our way up to having short conversations in which we discussed the weather or ordered lunch.

After an opening lecture, the teacher divided the class into thirds. With a sweep of her hand, she told my third to have a short story ready for the next class. I was panic-stricken. How could I write a story by next week? What *was* a story? Sure I had read some, whole books of them even, but I had also lived in houses all my life with only the vaguest notion about how to build one. Where would I get an idea? Once I had an idea, what should the first sentence be? The second? How many people should be in my story, and how much could they do? Could they fly to Nepal and climb a mountain, or should they just talk about going there while eating lunch? How would the story end?

That was my introduction to how a writer looks at fiction, at what the essential elements are, how they relate to each other, what must come first, second, and third. This is a different perspective from that of regular readers or even literature teachers. Readers and teachers are like visitors who've paid money to tour a famous home. Ah, readers say, what lovely rooms. Yes, the teacher says, notice the artful placement of the windows. Writers look at a story the way a carpenter or an architect looks at a house: They see the surface but also the structure under the paint. They know how the house is put together and how much work it was to build.

For me, desperation was a powerful source of inspiration. I did write a story. It took every free moment of that short week and a final forty-eight hours of agony hunched over a manual typewriter with

1

little bottles of Wite-Out (in those pre-computer days) to get the story ready to turn in. I discovered I did instinctively know what a story was. Why? Because narrative is in the bones of our culture and language. At each day's end we tell ourselves the story of what happened, and each morning at breakfast, we run through the likely plot of the new day. We also have an impulse toward fiction, toward rearranging events to make them more interesting, to give them more of a point or at least a punch line.

I did know what a story was, and I was able to write one. But I stumbled through that first attempt not knowing the most basic tricks of the trade. None of the decisions I made were wrong, but my lack of knowledge severely limited my choices. I wrote that first story because I didn't know how to write any other. While that might work once, I quickly realized I couldn't do the same thing over and over and hope for a lifetime of writing. I had to know more.

After my panic over that first story, I turned to the books on writing that were available, but I was often frustrated by their approach. Most seemed more suited to the study of literature, of stories already written, than to the concerns of a struggling writer. Others took a Chinese menu approach to the elements of fiction—choose one from column A, one from column B—as if each decision a writer made about a story stood alone, as if a writer could just choose any point of view, any method of characterization, without one element having an effect on another. I sensed even then that in fiction, as in a house, each element is part of the story's structure, that just as every board, rafter, and brick was intimately connected to the others, every choice a writer made along the way affected the whole story.

I kept writing and I kept learning, story by story and, later, novel by novel, until I had a range of techniques I could draw on to build my fiction. I learned that the point of view you choose determines what story you can tell, that conflict controls plot, that endings are built on the conflicts you establish. Now I can choose the structure I need to fit any story I might want to write. Most important, I learned how to make these elements work together, each adding to the beauty and effectiveness of the whole. These structural elements are the materials, framing lumber, tenpenny nails, door frames, and shingles I use to give my experiences and thoughts shape, to turn my imaginings into finished fiction. That is why I chose the title *Building Fiction*.

In the first nine chapters, I discuss where you can find the best materials for your fiction and the various plans you can follow and tools you can use to put a short story or novel together. I cover where ideas come from, openings for your fiction, the crucial question of point of view, effective characterization, the use of conflict, writing endings, and how to revise. Each subject is considered in the order it would come up in the writing of a single short story or novel, clearly showing how the structural elements are connected to each other and to the work as a whole. I provide plenty of examples from the best contemporary writing, my own work, and old favorites such as Charles Dickens and Jane Austen. The last three chapters of *Building Fiction* deal with the demands of specific fictional forms. One chapter is on the structural differences between the novel and the short story. Another covers the structure of the short short story, the novella, and the novel-in-stories. The final chapter is on experimental writing. There I'll show you when you can break, or at least bend, the practical structural rules you've just learned and still leave a story that works.

THE ELEMENTS
OF STRUCTURE

CHAPTER ONE

SOURCES FOR FICTION

T he most frightening task for any writer is getting started. Whether you are beginning your first short story or your fifth novel, that expanse of white space can seem as uncrossable as the high arctic in winter. The trick is to see that first blank page as a challenge. The famous architect Frank Lloyd Wright always visited the site for a proposed building before he drew up any plans, whether the structure was to be a civic center, an industrialist's mansion, or a simple summer cottage. He was inspired, he said, by the terrain. He always had ideas, theories, but nothing could be put into practice in the abstract. A building had to stand somewhere, and where it stood helped him determine the materials and method of construction.

Like Wright, you are an architect, a builder of fiction. What sites are available to you, and what materials do you have on hand? An architect brings his years of training, his lifelong experience of looking at and living in buildings, to his task. You, too, have resources waiting to be tapped. Although the page is still blank, your mind is full of places, people, events, and the words to describe them.

READING FOR IDEAS

The great Argentinean writer Jorge Luis Borges believed that we are most influenced by the books we read as children. For this reason he named Robert Louis Stevenson as his own strongest influence. The first place many writers turn to gather materials is the books they loved when they were young. Most writers were voracious readers as children.

If you weren't, it is too late to add or delete books from the library of your youth, but it helps to acknowledge the ones that are there.

And don't be a snob about it. I read everything from Ian Fleming's James Bond novels to the Hardy Boys, from C.S. Forester's Horatio Hornblower books to Charles Dickens' *Bleak House* and Fyodor Dostoyevsky's *Crime and Punishment,* without making much distinction between them. All had something to teach me about fiction. From James Bond I got my first forbidden taste of the heady combination of sex and violence that, for better or worse, is a major part of twentieth-century culture. From Hornblower I picked up how to make use of both continuing characters (the same captain and crew together on long cruises in book after book) and authentic detail (the novels could serve as textbooks on early-nineteenth-century naval warfare). From the Hardy Boys I discovered how to use mystery as a plot device. From Dickens I learned the joy of minor characters. Dostoyevsky taught me that all plot is a war for the soul. Make your own list of books, and see what they taught you.

What you read as a child is only the beginning. Now you must begin to read in a more systematic way. If you are writing a novel, then start reading them. Make a list of all the novels or authors you've always wanted to read but haven't gotten around to. Combine the old with the new: *Moby Dick* or *Jane Eyre* and something reviewed in last Sunday's *New York Times Book Review.* Ask friends what they are reading, or look at interviews with famous writers to see which books influenced them. Once you find writers you like, try reading everything they've written. Early novels are often instructive; even great writers started out as beginners. If there is a bookstore or college in your area where writers give readings from their works, go and listen. Often the authors take questions, and you can ask them for the stories behind their stories or for the names of their favorite writers.

If you want to write short stories, start reading them. A good place to begin exploring is in one of the anthologies used as texts in college classrooms. In addition to these, I suggest the annual prize collections, such as *The Best American Short Stories, Pushcart Prize, Prize Stories: The O. Henry Awards,* and *New Stories From the South,* all of which print their selections of the best works published in magazines the previous year. These collections include stories from the literary magazines. These magazines, such as the *Paris Review, Ploughshares, Story,* and *Mississippi Review*, are where fiction is happening right now.

Read books of short stories by a single author. It is instructive to study how the stories are arranged. Sometimes they share repeating characters or are linked by theme or place. Even if the stories have nothing in common but the author, they offer a chance to see how one person has solved the problem of what to write about and how to write about it, time and time again. There are many great writers who have written or are writing short stories. I have my favorites, but the best way is for you to start your own list of the authors whose work you enjoy in the anthologies, then go and get their books.

Finally, the books that can help you generate ideas for stories don't have to be fiction themselves. I used to write my early drafts on yellow legal pads in an obscure corner on the sixth floor of the college library. A decade or so earlier, the library had switched from the Dewey decimal to the Library of Congress catalogue system, and the sixth floor was where the overworked librarians had stuck all the books that didn't seem worth re-cataloguing. Most of these had been ordered in the days when the school was a women's college. Many had not been checked out since. Between drafts I used to poke around the dusty volumes. There were turn-of-the-century cookbooks, handbooks designed to explain the various orders of nuns to potential postulants, a great firsthand account by a warden of her days in charge of a women's prison. My curiosity paid off. I wrote a short story based on a guidebook to the 1904 St. Louis world's fair and another that quoted from a medieval bestiary. Poke around in the stacks. There are stories in the map room and among the home repair books, in today's newspaper, and in old ones you can read only on microfilm.

IDEAS FROM LANGUAGE

The most basic building materials of fiction are, of course, words. Plenty of people think they have great ideas for stories but complain, I think mistakenly, that they don't have the words to express them. Words filled the air around us from the moment of birth. Like the books you read as a child, the language spoken around you has already helped shape the writer you are or will become.

I was raised in the South, land of extravagant talkers, where a politician on the radio might say in answer to a charge his opponent made, "Why, that's like a bullfrog calling the alligator ugly." When I first moved to the Midwest, I was struck by how different the language was. If two people were standing in front of an elephant at the Milwaukee Zoo, they would tend to use repetition, not metaphor, for emphasis: "He's big," one might say. "Yep, big," the other. Then the first would repeat, "Big," with a curt nod by way of emphasis. This tendency makes my Midwestern students natural minimalists. Ernest Hemingway's writing is probably closer to their natural voice than William Faulkner's. On the other hand, the language they draw on has its own stark honesty and power. You tend to believe what they write.

Of course, my typecasting of language by region is a sweeping generalization. No matter where we are from, we all possess a range of voices. We speak differently to friends than to employers, write notes to tack up on the refrigerator in more colloquial language than we use on job applications. The trick is to find the best of your range for what you are writing and use it. If you choose a spoken voice, use one you know intimately. If a more elevated diction is called for, you must be at ease there, too. If you need inspiration for this, hit the street for some fresh air and pick up the slang you need. Or go to the library to absorb the language of geographers or philatelists if you need to. Think of Vladimir Nabokov learning to write beautifully first in French, then in English, after being raised speaking Russian. All of us start with our own voices, the language of our class and region, and by practice, as if we were singing scales, we expand our range.

Beware of Stale Ideas

As you gather the materials of writing, be careful about drawing on television and movies. When you rely too heavily on mass media, whose messages are available to almost everybody on the planet, it may be hard to write a story that will strike readers as fresh or original or worth their time. It's the difference between fresh and stale air. If you write a story about living in New York based solely on watching lots of Woody Allen movies or episodes of *NYPD Blue*, readers may think, *I know just as much about New York as this guy*, and they will, because they know it from the same secondhand sources.

Another problem with drawing on movies and television is that it underestimates the differences between visual and written forms. I often go to the theater with my husband, who is a photographer, and come out feeling as if we had seen two different movies. As a visual person, he is affected strongly by what he sees, the images glowing on the screen. He is interested in the set design, the cinematography, the way a movie looks. He will appreciate a movie that leaves me grousing about lousy dialogue, shallow characterization, and incomprehensible plot. Song lyrics that depend on the music to give them emotional resonance can seem flat or clichéd in print in a way that poetry doesn't. Likewise, television and movie plots can look out of place on the printed page.

IDEAS FROM LIFE

You cannot stop the books you've read and the shows you've seen from influencing the fiction you write. After all, loving those stories is probably one reason why you want to write your own. In the end, though, the strongest and most workable materials are close at hand and consist of all the sights, sounds, colors, smells, emotions, odd characters, and weird events you have experienced in your own life.

All the books, even this one, say to write what you know, but the problem is that you know too much. An entire life is usually too big a subject for a short story, too big even for a novel. To find useful material in your life, focus on memories that stand alone: hospital stays, visits by relatives, weddings, high school reunions, all-state wrestling tournaments, the day you met or left your first husband. These are the self-contained events that lend themselves to being made into stories.

Trips are perfect. They have a natural beginning, middle, and end, which can suggest the basic structure for your fiction. The idea for my story "Underground Women" came to me after seeing a woman collapse in a laundromat in Paris. I doubt I would have remembered every detail of the incident if it hadn't been part of an already memorable trip. In Canadian writer Alice Munro's wonderful short story "Miles City, Montana," a casual stop on a cross-country trip turns into the near drowning of the narrator's young daughter, an event that becomes the defining moment of her character's life.

Don't define your life too narrowly. Think of it as a river of stories flowing to you from your father, mother, aunts, uncles, sisters, brothers, and friends. A particularly good place to start is with your parents' or even your grandparents' lives. Writing about something that happened before you were born is a good antidote to the natural tendency to make yourself the center of attention. The danger isn't that you will be egotistical (all writers are egotists), but that you will neglect to tell your readers something essential because it seems too obvious. Besides, stories you have heard repeated in your family have already been distilled, boiled down to a potent essence. Also, since you often know only part of the story, you have the freedom to imagine the rest.

My mother-in-law once told me that during World War II she and her husband almost rented an abandoned lighthouse. They had moved to Staten Island where a housing shortage forced them to consider bizarre alternatives, but she had two small children and couldn't spend all her time going up and down such dangerously steep stairs. So they rented a basement apartment instead. After hearing this I immediately wanted to write a short story about a woman living in a lighthouse, not about my mother-in-law watching people's feet pass by outside her sidewalk-level window. That's the joy of fiction.

EXERCISES

Think of this set of exercises as preparation for (or continuation and nurturing of) the place writing fills in your life. Before the exercises, a simple set of ABCs.

A. Set aside a place to write. It should offer at least some privacy (a door between you and the world is nice), though a room of one's own, to borrow from Virginia Woolf, is not always possible. Try to find a spot where other work does not intrude. I try not to pay bills or grade papers in the same place I write, but if the kitchen table is the only desk you have, clear the dishes and make the best of it. These days you may be more likely to write at the nearest available computer than in a cozy chair by the fire. Wherever it is, find the space that works for you and guard it with your life.

B. Clear a shelf on your bookcase, preferably close to where you write. Fill it with books you love and books you will want to refer to as you write.

C. Buy a notebook, one small enough to carry around. In it make the following lists:

1. Your favorite books. Explore why you remember each one. Was it a particular scene? A character? A memorable phrase or insight into life?

2. Books you have always wanted to read. If you draw a blank or even if you don't, go to a bookstore or library and add at least ten more to your list. Go out of your way to visit the library's rare book room or a good used-book store. Go to a fiction reading or buy a literary magazine. Do it because you are a writer.

3. Ten expressions your mother/father/family/best friend uses regularly, especially those you don't hear anyone else use. For example, my mother used to say, " 'To each his own,' said the old lady as she kissed the cow."

4. Ten sentences you overhear in a day at work, on the street, or in the grocery store that catch your attention. Do it right then, like a stenographer or a spy. Also jot down any written language (signs or graffiti or names of stores) that catches your attention. Do this for a week.

5. Ten trips you've taken in your life from short (to the dentist) to long (to the Grand Canyon). Write at least one thing you remember seeing you doubt anyone else would have noticed on the same trip and one thought you remember having. Be specific. Head this list *Potential Story Ideas.*

6. Ten important occasions or events (weddings, graduations, funerals, office parties) from your life and what you remember about them. Include at least one statement you remember someone making. Add these to your list of Potential Story Ideas.

7. The facts of your parents' lives before you were born. Where did they grow up? Go to school? Live when you were born? What did they do on Saturday nights before you came along? These are also Potential Story Ideas.

8. Any family stories you have heard more than once. Are there stories about your own birth? Childhood? Don't forget the ones that make you cringe. Those may be your best Potential Story Ideas.

9. Ten ideas for stories based just on the titles or a few words of someone else's fiction. To generate this list, flip quickly through the books on your bookshelf or at the library. Here are still more Potential Story Ideas.

10. Every night for a week, ask yourself before you go to bed, What happened today that would make a good short story or part of a novel? Include things you remembered or were told as well as events you witnessed. Add these to your Potential Story Ideas list.

CHAPTER TWO

OPENINGS IN FICTION

L et's say your character wakes up and your story begins with the day, a natural and popular way to start. Too popular. A few years ago, a friend and fellow writer was the first reader of five hundred manuscripts sent in for a well-known book contest. She complained that half the stories opened with someone waking up. She complained so bitterly and so often, another friend couldn't resist the temptation to send a mock query letter asking if the contest had received her manuscript, *The Alarm Clock Rang and Other Stories*.

The real problem with beginning a story with your character flat on her back in bed isn't the alarm clock. It is what comes next. She has to get up, get dressed, and brush her teeth. In other words she has to make it through a great deal of relatively uninteresting stuff before her day and the real story take off. I learned this lesson when I was in that first writing class. My teacher read aloud a story by another student. It was a classic alarm clock opening (in this case a clock radio), but I was too new to fiction writing to recognize it. I was immediately drawn into the story by the wealth of detail. I was more than a little envious. Could I describe the shaving of a chin so vividly? Could I manage having a character read the morning paper and eat a waffle at the same time? After a while though, I felt my attention wander. I shifted in my seat. What was the story about? What did the character want? Would he ever get out of his house? Stories for this class were supposed to be ten pages long, and we were getting nowhere fast over that gloriously evoked waffle. By the end of page nine, it was clear that the author was running out of room and still hadn't found the story. On page ten our waffle eater walked out the front door and was struck down by a meteor. The class sat stunned for a moment, then groaned. We were only students, but we knew an act of desperation when we saw one.

Starting your story in bed may be a sign that you aren't sure of what your story is or where it is headed. It's as if you've opened the front door to reveal a hallway, a really big hallway, a place to hang coats and dripping umbrellas, then left your readers with no place to sit down in a room where not much is likely to happen. Even from the first few sentences, readers need to know that you know where you are taking them. How do writers do this? A good way to find out is to turn back to your bookshelf and read some first paragraphs of a short-story collection or novel. How much do you know after a half-dozen sentences? Can you guess where the plot is headed? By the end of the first paragraph of a short story or novel, we should have a strong feeling of the underlying structure. We should know that someone wants something and wants it badly. Desire creates conflict, and conflict is the heart of all fiction. We need to feel that something—something important—is just about to happen.

After reading the introductory paragraphs of a few stories and novels, you should be able to note similarities. You may find yourself saying, "This one starts with dialogue just like that one did." Structurally, openings tend to fall into three basic types, which I'll call *Into the Pot, Already Boiling*; *Calm Before the Story*; and *Opening Statements to the Jury*. All rules have exceptions, thank goodness, and any attempt to make an orderly business of the structure of fiction, let alone life, is bound to risk oversimplification in the name of illumination. But my general rule in this book is to allow myself any system of classification that I find useful as a fiction writer. I can only hope you find it helpful too.

INTO THE POT, ALREADY BOILING

This is the most common of all openings. In it the story or novel begins in midaction, in flight. The front door of the house opens to reveal a party in progress. The elevator doors whoosh apart to reveal two characters in the heated middle of an argument. What the argument appears to be about, let alone the subtleties of what it is *really* about, may not be immediately apparent, but readers, like all good eavesdroppers, get on the elevator hoping to find out.

Raymond Carver's "Are These Actual Miles?" is a good example of a short story that opens quickly.

> Fact is the car needs to be sold in a hurry, and Leo sends Toni out to do it. Toni is smart and has personality. She used to sell children's encyclopedias door to door. She signed him up, even though he didn't have kids. Afterward, Leo asked her for a date, and the date led to this. This deal has to be cash, and it has to be done tonight.

By the end of the first paragraph, we know what Leo and Toni want and want badly. They are headed for bankruptcy and need to sell the car before the court takes it away. By the end of the first page, it becomes clear that selling the car may involve Toni having sex with the buyer, and so we know there is no easy way for them to get what they want. We are hooked, and we have to read to the end of the story to find out what happens.

When a story or novel takes off with a bang, important facts are often held back for a paragraph or page. We have to puzzle out what the characters want. The trick is to make the puzzle interesting, one worth your readers' time and effort. Amy Hempel's "In the Cemetery Where Al Jolson Is Buried" begins with the sound everyone is naturally attuned to, the sound of the human voice.

> "Tell me things I won't mind forgetting," she said. "Make it useless stuff or skip it."
>
> I began. I told her insects fly through rain, missing every drop, never getting wet. I told her no one in America owned a tape recorder before Bing Crosby did. . . .
>
> The camera made me self-conscious and I stopped. It was trained on us from a ceiling mount—the kind of camera banks use to photograph robbers. It played our image to the nurses down the hall in Intensive Care.

Once Hempel has gone a little farther, dropping in more clues like the words *intensive care*, we begin to realize that the speaker of that opening line is dying. By then we are already deeply involved.

Novels often open with a flurry of characters in midaction. Over the course of the first few pages or the first chapter, the writer reveals to us those characters' desires and so sets in motion the conflict that is at the center of the story. Edith Wharton's classic novel *The House of Mirth* begins at a train station.

> Selden paused in surprise. In the afternoon rush of the Grand Central Station his eyes had been refreshed by the sight of Miss Lily Bart.
>
> It was a Monday in early September, and he was returning to his work from a hurried dip into the country, but what was Miss Bart doing in town at that season?

Only gradually do we learn that Lily Bart is a young woman from a good family who has no money and who must, by the social rules of the time, marry well to survive. More gradually still do we see how her meeting with Selden brings her to pass up a chance to marry, exiles her from society, and leads to her penniless death. All this from a meeting in a train station.

Sometimes a novel begins even more mysteriously in the middle of something we don't quite understand. The South African writer J.M. Coetzee's novel *Waiting for the Barbarians* opens someplace and sometime that can only be vaguely defined as the not here and not now.

> I have never seen anything like it: two little discs of glass suspended in front of his eyes in loops of wire. Is he blind? I could understand it if he wanted to hide blind eyes. But he is not blind. The discs are dark, they look opaque from the outside, but he can see through them. He tells me they are a new invention. "They protect one's eyes against the glare of the sun," he says. . . . "At home everyone wears them."

We read on, intrigued, and are led into a political allegory in which the narrator, the magistrate, a servant of an empire back home, must decide once and for all whom he serves.

Lead with a great line of dialogue or with a dramatic physical action, and readers will wait to find out that the speaker is dying, that the setting is the Gilded Age of the 1890s, or that they are in the desert outpost of an imaginary empire. I use an extreme form of this in my short story "Underground Women," which starts with a sort of snapshot, a visual set piece, that catches the reader's attention but only hints at the identity of the speaker, a young American girl.

> I am taking a photograph of a Lavomatic near the Gare du Nord in Paris. It will be a color photograph and so will show the walls sharp yellow, the machines the shiny white that means clean. The front of the Lavomatic is plate glass. Glass that lets out into the night the bright fluorescent light of the laundry. Glass that reflects a red hint of an ambulance beacon. Glass that lets the photographer catch this scene, this knot of official people grouped casually around a dark wrinkled shape on the floor. Catch at an angle of extreme foreshortening the stubby, already almost blue legs, the one outflung hand holding one black sock.
>
> It will be the photograph of a dead woman.

I could have begun with dialogue or with a camera clicking or even with the next sentence of the short story: "It is on the evening of my first day in Paris that I take the photograph of the dead woman in the Lavomatic and then check into Le Grand Hotel de l'Univers Nord." But the photograph of the dead woman is the central image in the short story, and by introducing the story with such a graphic and detailed description of the photo, I am telling my readers that.

Later when I decided to expand "Underground Women" into the novel *The Museum of Happiness*, many things changed, including the first scene, but again I chose to open in midaction. I stayed with Into the Pot, Already Boiling.

> In the morgue, Ginny Gillespie took a step forward and laid a finger on her husband Paul's cheek, touched a corner of his mouth where death had caught him blank-faced, too busy to smile or frown. His skin felt like wet rubber, like a hand hidden in a surgeon's glove. It was October 5, 1929. Ginny had only been married to Paul for three months.

In an earlier draft, the novel had begun with a neighbor bringing Ginny the news that her husband had died suddenly, but I decided while revising to cut those pages. Start in the morgue, my instincts told me, and most readers will keep reading at least long enough to find out how Paul died.

CALM BEFORE THE STORY

At first glance the Calm Before the Story opening can look a great deal like The Alarm Clock Rang. People sit in rocking chairs or car seats, look out windows. Scenery is described. But readers know that a good story is never about a perfectly still summer day in which nothing happens. Tension is created because they are sure something important is about to. This is why the class all listened carefully to the initial paragraphs of the waffle-eating short story before drifting off. The trick with Calm Before the Story openings is to delay in the hallway just long enough to generate tension, then open the door to the living room and the main action, to reveal the conflict before you lose readers' attention. In a novel, the Calm Before the Story may appear in a foreword or take up part or all of chapter one. In a short story, it usually lasts no longer than the second paragraph or the second page. If I had begun "Underground Women" with an idyllic account of an evening stroll through Paris, City of Light, before meeting the dead woman in the Lavomatic on page two, it would be a classic case of Calm Before the Story.

Sometimes the subject of a short story or novel makes clear the calm is bound to be broken by violence or storm. *All Quiet on the Western Front*, novelist Erich Maria Remarque's wrenchingly realistic novel of German soldiers in the trenches during World War I, opens with just such a passage.

> We are at rest five miles behind the front. Yesterday we were relieved, and now our bellies are full of beef and haricot beans. We are satisfied and at peace. Each man has another mess-tin full for the evening; and, what is more, there is a double ration of sausage and bread. That puts a man in fine trim. We have not had such luck as this for a long time. The cook with his carroty head is begging us to eat; he beckons with his ladle to every one that passes, and spoons him out a great dollop. He does not see how he can empty his stewpot in time for coffee.

These men are combatants in one of the bloodiest wars in history, and this litany of small comforts, so lovingly recounted, only makes it seem inevitable to readers that great hardships are coming. The peace here is not real peace, no matter what the narrator says in this moment.

Whenever an author or a character seems to dwell on a certain mood a bit too long, readers suspect the opposite is true. If the author of The Alarm Clock Rang short story in my first writing class had known in advance (or in a subsequent revision) that his character was headed for death at the hands of the cosmos, he could have created tension in an otherwise tensionless short story by stressing how perfect the morning was, how perfect the waffle was, how nothing could spoil it.

OPENING STATEMENTS TO THE JURY

Some stories begin not with action or description but with thematic statements in which an author or character makes explicit just what is at stake and what the conflict is. This is a less common opening, but one that can be very effective, especially in establishing early that the issue is larger than readers might otherwise assume.

A wonderful example of the opening thematic statement occurs in Joy Williams' short story "Taking Care." Jones, the central character, is a minister. He is taking care of his dying wife and of a child left in his charge by his absent daughter. But more than the physical wants of others is at stake here. Williams spells that out from the first sentence.

> Jones, the preacher, has been in love all his life. He is baffled by this because as far as he can see, it has never helped anyone, even when they have acknowledged it, which is not often. Jones's love is much too apparent and arouses neglect. He is like an animal in a traveling show who, through some aberration, wears a vital organ outside the skin, awkward and unfortunate, something that shouldn't be seen, certainly something that shouldn't be watched working.

Love and its meaning are on trial, Williams is telling her readers. If she had not used the initial thematic statement, the opening scene at the wife's bedside in the hospital might have set up a more worldly, less spiritual expectation. Ah, readers might say, this is about physical health, and the point will be whether or not the wife gets well.

Another short story that uses the same technique is Robin Hemley's "The Mouse Town."

Mitch and I were friends by pure chance, and the wonderful world of torture might never have opened up to us if not for the deaths of our fathers. After all, we were the only kids at Pitman Elementary School with dead dads, though they had died in different ways.

Without this introduction the first scene of the two boys torturing a pet mouse by making him view his "dead father" at a paper funeral home would be just horrifying instead of an effective mix of painful and deeply touching.

Novels, too, can have thematic openings. Ford Madox Ford's classic novel *The Good Soldier* begins in just such a way.

This is the saddest story I have ever heard. We had known the Ashburnhams for nine seasons of the town of Nauheim with an extreme intimacy—or, rather, with an acquaintance-ship as loose and easy and yet as close as a good glove's with your hand. My wife and I knew Captain and Mrs. Ashburnham as well as it was possible to know anybody, and yet, in another sense, we knew nothing at all about them.

This is a particularly risky way to start a story. All comedians know the danger of announcing to an audience that they are going to tell them the funniest joke they have ever heard, and for Ford Madox Ford to begin with his narrator saying this is going to be the saddest story, risks our deciding it is not sad at all. But as in "Taking Care" or "The Mouse Town," the opening proves essential to our under-standing. By the end of the book, we realize the absolute truth of the first sentence.

I could have started "Underground Women" with a thematic state-ment. I felt when I was writing it—and still believe—that the short story is about the poor way women are treated in this world and about their solidarity in the face of such treatment. But just saying that flat out, in print here, makes me cringe. I can't help feeling that some readers would be unlikely to finish a short story beginning with a sentence like "This is a story about what happens to women in this world." There are more subtle ways of stating that theme, but rightly or wrongly, I decided to start with action and visual imagery and let them carry the story. Reservations, such as mine, are why the Opening Statement to the Jury, while effective, is used less often than the other two types of openings.

WRITE, THEN REWRITE

After reading all this advice on openings, you may be too frightened to write at all, so a word of reassurance. The short-story writer and novelist Marly Swick says she often starts without knowing what the second word, let alone the second sentence or paragraph or page will be. She just keeps asking herself, What could happen that would be interesting? And after that, What could happen to make what came before even more interesting? In other words she discovers her opening on the page then just keeps moving, writing her way deeper and deeper into her story, working out the structure as she goes.

So pick an opening. Get someone moving or shouting, set a peaceful scene, or state a theme. If the story continues to interest you enough to carry it through to the end, you can always rewrite the beginning. Great openings are made in revision. So get going and see where that first word leads you. When you finish the first draft, flip immediately back to page one and ask yourself, Is this still the right opening? If it is, rewrite it until every word pulls your readers into the story.

RED LIGHTS AND WARNING SIGNS

The beginning of a story deserves special care and attention because it introduces readers to everything that follows. If you think of the opening as a first date or a job interview, the importance of making a good impression becomes clear. You wouldn't walk into someone's office without so much as a hello or a handshake. The opening of your story is that hello to your readers. You want your handshake to be firm and convincing.

When I was a student at the Iowa Writers' Workshop, a well-known editor came to give a special workshop. He had chosen a student's short story in advance to talk about. All of fifty fiction students squeezed into the faculty lounge clutching our photocopies of the short story, waiting to hear him talk. The student whose work was the object of all this attention perched nervously in the front row. As it turned out, he had reason to be nervous.

The short story was about a long car trip to and through Lion Country Safari. The central character was an unhappy man trapped on a disaster date with a woman and her young sons. The editor tore into the first paragraph, objecting to a line about the car having stopped at ten or fifteen red lights. "How can I trust an author who can't count?" the editor said. I thought he was wrong. Who keeps a precise count of stoplights? Especially beyond, say, three. And why not just take the uncertainty as a sign of the personality of the central character, the poor put-upon guy? More than wrong, I thought he was being silly. Readers would never stop trusting an author over just a red light or two, would they?

I'm still not sure the editor was right about the red lights, but now I know he saw them as a sign of potential trouble ahead, in the same way I've come to take alarm clocks as the sign of a story that may end without ever truly getting started. How sure is this author of her story? How much does she deserve my time and attention? By now I have also done enough editing myself to know how a small glitch, slip, or rough spot in a first paragraph is often all the excuse you need to put a story down, to reject it, and go on to the next one.

EXERCISES

1. Read the beginning paragraph of a story, then stop and write what you think the story is going to be about. Now read the rest. Were you right?

2. Reread the first page of a novel you know well. How does that page shape your expectation of what will happen in the rest of the novel?

3. Rewrite the opening paragraph of a story or page of a novel you have read. If it is an Into the Pot, Already Boiling, try a thematic Opening Statement to the Jury. If it is a Calm Before the Story, try cutting to the chase with an Into the Pot, Already Boiling opening.

4. Rewrite the opening paragraph of a story you have written or page one of your novel. Try switching it from one type to another— for example, from Calm Before the Story to Opening Statements to the Jury. Try making it more true to its type.

5. Write openings to ten stories or novels you might write, being sure to try all three types. You can use the list of Potential Story Ideas you generated in the last chapter. Don't worry about whether you are really going to write the rest of the story or novel, but do try to write openings that are immediate and gripping.

CHAPTER THREE

THIRD-PERSON POINT OF VIEW

Every writer has a theory about which of the many decisions that go into writing a short story or a novel is the most important. That's one reason why it's a good idea to read more than one writing book like this. Each element of fiction helps determine the overall structure, to make the story you are building both functional and distinctive. But I will be up front about one of my obsessions: I think *point of view* is the heart of narrative. For me it's the foundation of fiction; everything else rests on it. If you decide to change the point of view of a finished story, you will find yourself making major alterations, not just minor sentence-by-sentence adjustments, because the change is not cosmetic. It is structural. Many people who are not writers, and far too many writers, think of point of view as a minor technical decision, something to fine-tune later, like which typeface to use. But it is really the choice of who tells us your story, and that determines what story you can tell. In this chapter and the next, we'll cover what you'll need to choose the right viewpoint for your fiction.

In literature classes, point of view is usually handled as a game of spot-the-pronoun. We are taught that stories and novels with a surplus of *I* are in first person; *he, she,* or *we*, third person; and *you*, second. We are given examples that prove this.

> [THIRD PERSON] The bride was trying to get dressed, but it wasn't working. There were just too many little buttons, and her hands were shaking. "I guess I'm nervous," she said.

[FIRST PERSON] I couldn't believe my own grandmother would drink so much. "Don't you want to lie down, Granny?" I asked, sounding patient and sweet, but I felt like shooting her.

[SECOND PERSON] All the relatives that you never met before, the really strange ones, are crowding around and suddenly Grandma is swinging a bottle and shouting. You get up and look for an exit. A cigarette would be good.

The analysis of possible points of view for this wedding gone bad looks easy because these are simple examples. In practice each alternative has enough possible variations to greatly complicate the issue, especially when you are deciding which one to use in a short story or novel you are writing. From just these examples, you can see that point of view strongly affects what kind of wedding tale is told. As we move through these next two chapters, I'll keep returning to this fictional wedding, showing how each approach would affect this one potential story. Because third person has the most variations, I'll discuss it in this chapter and leave first and second person for the next.

Whichever option you do choose, you must stick to it consistently. Slipping from one to another inadvertently will unnerve your readers. They will simply stop trusting you.

HE, SHE, AND SOMETIMES THEY

Third person is by far the most common choice for point of view in the novel. A quick look at a recently published anthology of short stories shows fully two-thirds of them are written in third person, too. One reason for this is literary convention, but another is the versatility of this viewpoint. Writers have been working in third person long enough to develop techniques within it for telling almost any story. Beginning writers are often frightened by third person, which seems in its nearly infinite varieties to be too complicated to take on. Partly this is because the very term *third-person point of view* is a big box into which a number of rather different kinds of points of view get tossed. If we take the time to understand the possibilities within third person, while shopping for just the right one for our wedding story, it will seem less intimidating.

OMNISCIENT POINT OF VIEW

Why limit yourself to human wedding guests? Why not start at the top? You could tell the story of the wedding from a third-person omniscient point of view. The traditional explanation is that this is like telling a story from God's viewpoint or at least with the benefit of divine powers. In a true omniscient, you can go into any character's mind and bring your readers along. You could go into the mind of each member of the family at the wedding. You could go into the minister's mind, the limousine driver's, even the tiny brains of the pigeons that come to eat the birdseed thrown at the departing couple.

In omniscient point of view, you have complete freedom in time and space. You can use this talent to tell us what is going on in any room of the church before, during, and after the wedding or in any room of any building on the planet. You could use these powers to report what the father of the bride says to his third wife, the bride's stepmother, and what she snaps back; to show us Uncle Henry getting drunk, as usual, out in the parking lot; to warn us the church's water heater is about to explode in the basement. You can do this by moving into a character's mind who knows these facts or who hears and sees what is happening, or you can do it by reporting directly to the readers. You can make more extravagant use of this freedom. You could tell us what weddings were like in Babylon in 3800 B.C., what they will be like on the moon, what our bride's first minutes in the world were like, moments of which she has no conscious memory, or what words she will utter on her death bed, an event decades in her future.

In addition the author using an omniscient point of view can make pronouncements that are meant to be taken by readers as unconditionally true. This voice, coming directly from the all-powerful creator of this particular fictional universe, is called *authorial voice*. You may ask readers to accept a small idea: "It was April, but unusually cold for that time of year." You can also make grander pronouncements, like opening a story with the sentence "Weddings are occasions of great happiness that lead, more often than not, to greater sorrow." Readers are supposed to nod at your wisdom, not protest your cynicism. An effective authorial voice also can help unify a tale, creating a clearer sense of connectedness.

The omniscient viewpoint is more common in novels than in stories. Novels by their very size often have a larger cast of characters and more physical and emotional territory to cover. By using omniscience, the novelist establishes the scope of the work. Many novels with this godlike perspective, in which the author dips in and out of the consciousness of a wide range of characters, announce the size of their intentions in their titles, such as William Thackeray's *Vanity Fair*, Leo Tolstoy's *War and Peace*, and Fyodor Dostoyevsky's *Crime and Punishment*.

However, a fully omniscient point of view is possible in a short story, too. "Fever Flower," by Shirley Ann Grau, opens with the authorial voice telling us, "Summers, even the dew is hot," and that same voice goes on to show us what is what in this small town.

> In the houses air-conditioning units buzz twenty-four hours a day. And colored laundresses grumble at the size of washes. . . . Nurses feed children perfunctory breakfast: cold cereals and juices at eleven o'clock. Summer mornings no one gets up early.

At the bottom of the first page after a little white space, we encounter our first named character. We start on the outside: "By eight-thirty Katherine Fleming was sitting alone in the efficient white and yellow tiled kitchen. . . ." Then we dip lightly into her thoughts: "She leaned her elbow on the counter, remembered the spilled juice and lifted her arm hastily. . . ." Soon we go deeper still: "It always annoyed her to lie." Later the author jumps forward in time to tell us what waits in the future for divorced Katherine.

> After a few more years she would find she much preferred a solitary day in town. After a few years she would find a positive pleasure in being alone.

By the end of the short story, the author has given Katherine's ex-husband and her daughter's nurse the same treatment, showing us what they do, say, and think in a given day as well as predicting their future.

Perfect, you might think, that's the point of view for me. The idea of being God, even of a universe the size of a single short story or book, has an undeniable appeal. But one problem with omniscience is that contemporary readers have a high resistance to godlike pronouncements, at least when they come from merely human authors.

One small example of this is the resistance you may have felt to Shirley Ann Grau's use of the world *colored* to describe the laundresses. It's understandable language in a short story first published in the 1950s but hard to take from our omniscient author.

In general the trend in literature in the last five hundred years has been from the high to the low. Traditionally only the highborn could fall far enough to justify a story being written detailing the events that led so inevitably to their death or disgrace. Oedipus is a king, Roland a count, and Hamlet a prince. By this century, however, Arthur Miller could write a play based on the final fall of an ordinary man, and audiences had no problem finding Willy Loman tragic at the end of *Death of a Salesman*. So like a king under a constitutional monarchy, the writer in the twentieth century has usually chosen to voluntarily surrender some of his powers in order to be closer to the people, to have their ear and their sympathy. The question to ask yourself is which of these third-person authorial powers you can surrender and still be able to tell your story.

1. the ability to go into any character's mind
2. complete freedom in time and space
3. the ability to have a separate authorial voice that can tell your readers truths, large and small

OBJECTIVE POINT OF VIEW

If modern readers have lost faith in omniscience—all-knowing as well as all-seeing—maybe, you think, I could settle for just all-seeing. One apt analogy for this point of view is the author as Big Brother. Maybe it would be enough to just see and hear everything that happens at the wedding, as if there were surveillance cameras mounted on the walls, microphones hidden in the wedding cake and in certain strategically chosen canapés. If readers could watch the wedding themselves, you could tell your story without going into any of the character's minds, leaving the church or reception hall, jumping backward or forward in time, or making any philosophical or meteorological pronouncements from on high.

This cameralike perspective is known as *objective point of view*. It's a variation of third person that comes naturally to a generation raised on film and video. "Just the facts, ma'am," as Joe Friday used to say on *Dragnet*. Its very narrowness creates a streamlined, efficient narrative structure, no wandering into strange settings or stray characters' heads. In practice, though, a totally objective viewpoint is rare. The example always cited is Ernest Hemingway's "Hills Like White Elephants," and this is because it's hard to come up with other pure examples of the form. The short story starts with a description of the setting.

> The hills across the valley of the Ebro were long and white. On this side there was no shade and no trees and the station was between two lines of rails in the sun.

The first thing you may notice about these sentences is that there is still a clear authorial voice. It is this voice that tells us there is no shade. In the objective point of view, the authorial voice limits itself to statements of description, taking the place of the opening panning shot in a movie and avoiding the larger philosophical pronouncements permissible in an omniscient point of view. The author is lying low, but he is still there. He is choosing what readers see just as the director makes choices in a movie or as Uncle Henry does with the video camera at a wedding. No film, no story, not even a novel as long as Marcel Proust's seven-volume *Remembrance of Things Past* has room for all of reality, for everything that happens. Even Big Brother cannot see or make readers see everything at once. The art of art is selection, and the author, though he may hide, is still running the show.

In the second paragraph of "Hills Like White Elephants," we hit our first line of dialogue, the most essential tool of the objective point of view. Dialogue makes readers feel they are there, listening in on real people.

> "What should we drink?" the girl asked. She had taken off her hat and put it on the table.
> "It's pretty hot," the man said.

But, again, just because the author is hidden doesn't mean he isn't there. This is not really a conversation we happen to overhear as we linger at a train station in Spain. It is only a short story pretending to be one. Hemingway has to succeed in telling us a story. A random slice of life might have no significance, but fiction is more carefully stage-managed than that. By the time Hemingway is done, he has managed to let us know that the girl who took off her hat is pregnant by the man who thinks it is hot, and that she is about to have an abortion. He is able to convey the decisive importance of this moment in his characters' lives, even though the characters themselves resist this realization. That is a lot to get across with nothing but terse dialogue and some dry, hot scenery.

Hemingway, through careful selection of dialogue and detail, tells his story within this extremely limiting point of view, with both legs and one arm, so to speak, tied behind his back. It takes special skills, but it can be done, and the results are elegantly beautiful. Similarly, a viewpoint that doesn't allow us access to the minds of either of the two central characters and that glues us to one spot in time and in space has some powerful strengths. It gives the story a distinctive, claustrophobic concentration, and the very tightness of the structure makes it memorable.

Is this difficult point of view the choice for you? Some contend even Hemingway slipped up a couple of times. "He looked up the track but could not see the train," Hemingway writes. Is the author telling what the character can and can't see from external appearances, or has he briefly slipped into the character's consciousness? (After looking up the track, the character walks back into the bar, an action that implies the train is not about to arrive.) This argument may be of interest only to scholars, but I prefer to take this small controversy as a sign of how hungry readers are for a glimpse inside these characters. Part of us wants Hemingway to give up his noble experiment in objectivity and tell the whole story. In life we can never truly know what it is like to be another person. We are locked inside our own heads with no way out. Third-person point of view in fiction exists so we can experience an approximation of another human's deepest thoughts, memories, and desires. Fiction, alone among the narrative arts, can move with such ease into a character's mind. It should come as no surprise that that power is one most authors surrender with the greatest reluctance.

This doesn't mean that an objective viewpoint can't work. After all, "Hills Like White Elephants" is probably Hemingway's most widely reprinted short story. Or that it doesn't have lessons to teach. If you take the time to think carefully how your story could be written from this point of view, you will realize how much of the story can be conveyed by action, description, and dialogue. This is invaluable, even if you end up adding a character's thoughts to the mix.

That is an approach the contemporary short-story writer Ann Beattie often uses. "Winter, 1978" starts with what appears to be an objective point of view.

> The canvases were packed individually, in shipping cartons. Benton put them in the car and slammed the trunk shut.
>
> "They'll be all right?" the man asked.
>
> "They survived in the baggage compartment of a 747, they'll do okay in the trunk," Benton said.
>
> "I love his work," the man said to Nick.
>
> "He's great," Nick said, and felt like an idiot.

It isn't until we hit the last line, where Nick feels like an idiot, that we realize the scene is from his point of view. Even then, for the rest of the short story, Beattie sticks largely to what appears to be an impersonal viewpoint, only occasionally dipping lightly into Nick's thoughts. She lets the objective descriptions of action and the dialogue carry almost all the weight of the story. Her example, with its third-person point of view mixing detachment with occasional glimpses into one character's mind, may be a more useful one to you than Hemingway's. It is an extreme form of the next category to be discussed.

LIMITED OMNISCIENT POINT OF VIEW

Most writing books list this as the most common variety of the third-person point of view, and they are right. But one reason is that the term *limited omniscient*, like *third person* itself, is a catchall. Technically, it refers to any viewpoint in which the author is using a less-than-complete range of omniscient powers, but it doesn't specify exactly which powers the author gives up. In this sense even objective point of view could be viewed as merely a form of the limited omniscient. In practice the term usually means that the author has kept a restricted authorial voice to be used for description or simple narration, along with the ability to go deeply into one or more of his characters' minds. In a short story, the author's choice is often to stick close to a single character. In a novel the choice to use several characters, a technique called *multiple point of view*, is more common.

Grandma

Limited omniscience generally confines the use of authorial voice to scene setting and basic narration. In short stories this is often limited to the first paragraph, and in novels, to chapter openings or transitions. So whether Grandma spends the whole wedding drinking champagne in her wheelchair or is free to roam the church and the reception hall in search of relatives to criticize, the most important idea to remember is that if the story is told from her point of view, we are largely limited to what she has some way of knowing.

For example, from the grandmother's perspective, we cannot know for certain how the bride is feeling, though the grandmother can observe the bride's behavior as well as report anything she might say. As someone who knows her granddaughter, she can also make judgments and assumptions based on what she sees and hears, but she may be misguided or entirely wrong. She is not the author, and so her word and her judgments do not have to be taken as gospel. If she says, "There is no such thing as a sad wedding," even though she has just seen her granddaughter weeping with an intensity that belies a mere case of prenuptial jitters, we readers are free to feel she is mistaken and be certain that we know more than she does.

Herein lies the delightful complexity of the limited omniscient point of view: The author can carefully let readers in on a secret, on a reality that eludes the point-of-view character. This can be the very reason to choose this approach. The more the tipsy grandmother rejoices in spite of the tears, raised voices, and broken champagne glasses, the more we are sure the wedding is a disaster in the making. This is the sort of tension of which stories are made.

On a more mundane, technical level, limiting yourself to the grandmother means you can't go places she is unlikely to visit, ruling out hearing what the best man and the groom say to each other in the men's room. If such a device turns out to be essential to your story, stop to consider that having Granny press her ear to the bathroom wall to overhear a crucial, last-minute confession may be less a sign of clever plotting and more a sign that you have chosen the wrong set of eyes and ears. Maybe Grandpa would have been a better choice.

If we do stick with the grandmother as our point-of-view character, her thoughts and memories will be available to us. Who she is and who she once was will shape our story. Since she has been to many weddings, we might assume she will naturally compare this one to others, perhaps her daughter's (the bride's mother) or her own. She can do this through dialogue, telling other characters what she thinks.

> "I don't think those pink gowns on the bridesmaids are near as nice as the green and red ones at Kendra's wedding last Christmas," Grammy Bigalow said, peering over her bifocals.

We can also move into her head to listen to her thoughts.

> *I was a prettier bride by a long shot*, Grammy thought. *Not that I'd tell poor dear Ellen, but the girl looks like a cart horse in that dress.*

Think of this interior dialogue as floating on the surface of someone's consciousness. The language in these verbalized thoughts usually reflects the spoken vocabulary and speech patterns of a character's dialogue. If Grammy uses *ain't* and *y'all* when she speaks, she probably does when she talks to herself, too.

There are at least two levels of thought below this. The first, one we've already seen in "Fever Flower," is where feelings that are not quite conscious are put into words by the author, not the character. Often these take the form of summary statements like, "She hated to lie." Our grandmother might think, "She hated the way her memory played tricks on her." The language for these thoughts usually reflects the descriptive authorial voice, though the movement from the verbalized level to this deeper one can be subtle and often permits some colloquialisms or dialect typical of the character's speech to appear in a modified form, as in this slight variation, "She *surely did* hate the way her memory played tricks on her."

Below this level of feelings translated into simple statements by the author lies the vast territory of the unconscious. Here thoughts are too deep for simple words, making this the territory of metaphor and image. The author could begin with, "She hated the way her memory played tricks on her," and then go farther.

> She hated the way words and names disappeared like rabbits down a hole just when she wanted them. Like Alice down the rabbit hole, she was falling, always falling.

Grandmother could reasonably be expected to know about rabbits, even about *Alice's Adventures in Wonderland*, but since the presumption is that the author is supplying the images and metaphors necessary to translate the essentially untranslatable, these images and metaphors don't have to be ones that would come naturally to a grandmother. Although she feels these things, she would not articulate them this way.

In Pulitzer prize-winning novelist William Kennedy's *Ironweed*, the central character, Francis, is not well educated. He is a bum, and when Francis speaks he sounds like one. But he is capable of great and deep emotions, and so Kennedy steps in to supply the language necessary to bring these feelings to life. As the author, he is free to use a word like *diurnal* even if it is not one Francis would use in speaking or even know.

> Francis, wearing his new socks, was first out of the mission, first to cast an anxious glance around the corner of the building at Sandra, who sat propped where he had left her, her eyes sewn as tightly closed by the darkness as the eyes of a diurnal bird. Francis touched her firmly with a finger and she moved, but without opening her eyes. He looked up at the full moon, a silver cinder illuminating this night for bleeding women and frothing madmen, and which warmed him with the enormous shadow it thrust forward in his own path. When Sandra moved he leaned over and put the back of his hand against her cheek and felt the ice of her flesh.

Farther down this road lies the technique known as *stream of consciousness*, in which there is no separate authorial voice. We swirl through the layers of consciousness as if we were a trout fly on the end of that expert fisherman's, the author's, rod. (For more about stream of consciousness, see chapter twelve.) This technique is used brilliantly by Virginia Woolf in her novel *Mrs. Dalloway* to take us deep into the scattered mind of her central character. The novel opens with preparations for a party and a single external detail, "Mrs. Dalloway said she would buy the flowers herself," and then goes into Mrs. Dalloway's mind as if off a diving board.

> For Lucy had her work cut out for her. The doors would be taken off their hinges; Rumpelmayer's men were coming.

> And then, thought Clarissa Dalloway, what a morning—fresh as if issued to children on a beach.
>
> What a lark! What a plunge! For so it had always seemed to her, when, with a little squeak of the hinges, which she could hear now, she had burst open the French windows and plunged at Bourton into the open air. How fresh, how calm, stiller than this of course, the air was in the early morning; like the flap of a wave; the kiss of a wave; chill and sharp and yet (for a girl of eighteen as she then was) solemn, feeling as she did, standing there at the open window, that something awful was about to happen; looking at the flowers, at the trees with the smoke winding off them and the rooks rising, falling; standing and looking until Peter Walsh said, "Musing among the vegetables?"—was that it?—"I prefer men to cauliflowers"—was that it?

We, too, could try going deeper and farther afield in Granny's mind at the wedding, leaving the clear realms of her experience.

> Words, words, words, with no rational connection to each other, spilling, bleeding, red poppies on a dying field. Life one long surrealist game, a long rainy Sunday afternoon spent playing Exquisite Corpse with people she wasn't sure she ever knew.

She could think this even though she doesn't have any idea who the surrealists were or how to play their automatic word games. We could keep going, mixing memory and sensation to capture the flow of the grandmother's thoughts as Virginia Woolf does with Mrs. Dalloway. But most writers would start back up out of the depths of Granny's mind after the reference to Alice in Wonderland and head for the surface, to the realm of the observable, returning to dialogue and action.

These trips into a character's mind and back out again often take place in the space of a single paragraph or page or chapter. Then the pattern is repeated. Although it sounds silly, I find it helpful to think of the layers of a character's mind as a *consciousness sandwich*. First comes the bread, usually physical action, *Granny leaned forward to whisper in Mrs. Mortonson's ear*, or dialogue, *"Is that piano in tune?"*

Then comes the lettuce, interior monologue: *Why do I bother to talk to Mary Mortonson? she thought. Everybody knew she was deaf as an andiron.* Next comes the tomato, summary general feelings: *She didn't like sitting with all the other useless old widows.* Then we reach the meat, translated unconscious thought: *She felt like an old rag doll tossed to one side, her head all cotton batting, her sawdust soul leaking away, little by little.* Finally we come back out to the bread, action or dialogue: *She sneezed hard and reached for her handkerchief. "Damn," she said.*

This pattern you will see repeated over and over in stories and novels. With a little practice, it will become almost as natural for you to navigate your character's thoughts as your own.

Little Sister

If you choose the bride's younger sister to be your eyes and ears, you also shape your story. By choosing a child, you gain a fresh view of the world and its adult complications. We tend to instinctively believe what children tell us. But the essential question here is, How young? If you decide to tell a story from the point of view, and thus the mind, of a six-year-old, you are setting yourself a daunting task. It is possible if you have a strong, separate authorial voice, one that can set the scene as Hemingway does in "Hills Like White Elephants," and if you are willing to do a more than usual amount of translating of nonverbal thoughts, as Kennedy does in *Ironweed*. If the sister is twelve, your task will be easier. At that age she is likely to see, and see through, everybody at the wedding, and her speech and thoughts are more likely to interest adult readers.

Noted Southern writer Carson McCullers chose this age for Frankie, the point-of-view character in her novel *The Member of the Wedding*.

> It happened that green and crazy summer when Frankie was twelve years old. This was the summer when for a long time she had not been a member. She belonged to no club and was a member of nothing in the world. Frankie had become an unjoined person who hung around in doorways, and she was afraid.

Notice how McCullers makes clear exactly how old Frankie is in the first sentence of the novel. This is a necessity with a young point-of-view character, one best gotten out of the way early either by stating an age or giving a grade in school (though this requires a bit of math from the readers, *Oh, if she's in sixth grade, she must be eleven. Or is that twelve?*). Otherwise their energy is diverted into a sideshow guessing game. *She sounds thirteen,* they'll think. *No, no, she's not wearing a bra. Ten?* Uncertainty like this makes readers grumpy and restless, putting them in the mood to question everything else in the story as well.

In McCullers' short story, Frankie learns that her brother is getting married, and she imagines the wedding.

> She saw a silent church, a strange snow slanting down against the colored windows. The groom in this wedding was her brother, and there was a brightness where his face should be. The bride was there in a long white train, and the bride also was faceless. There was something about this wedding that gave Frankie a feeling she could not name.

After this, her sister-in-law-to-be accuses her of being jealous, establishing one of the central tensions in the story. Perhaps that will be the tension in your wedding story, too. This is a perfect example of what a writer gains by using a young narrator. If Frankie were older, this passage would not be as effective. She is at the perfect age to be completely honest with the readers about her feelings even though she, herself, does not completely understand them.

Dog

There are other less obvious and perhaps more inherently odd choices for point of view. I have read stories written from the perspective of a pet rock, a portrait hanging on a wall, and a now-too-small dress hanging in a fat woman's closet. I can't honestly say the pet rock made a great point-of-view character (let's say it had a limited range of emotion), but if you choose to tell the story of the wedding from the viewpoint of old Aunt Alice's Seeing Eye dog, you will not be the first author to choose a mammal other than a human to carry your story. There is a long, honorable tradition of stories from the animal's perspective, one stretching back at least as far as Aesop's fables and probably, in oral tradition, to the oldest, firelit tales of the hunt. Jack London's point-of-view character in the classic nature novel *The Call of the Wild* is a half St. Bernard and half Scotch shepherd named Buck. Whether animal, vegetable, or mineral, be sure your eyes and ears can be where you need them, when you need them. If you choose Grandfather Brambley's portrait over the fireplace, you can't tell us about what happened at the wedding unless someone tells someone else all about the ceremony while warming his hands over the fire. If everyone does have to arrive in the parlor on a series of chilly nights to tell their sad, family tales, the choice of point of view is clearly determining both your plot and structure.

Photographer

If the wedding photographer were our eyes and ears in the story, you would have chosen a peripheral point-of-view character. This means your story would be one based on an outsider's version of the big day. When choosing a peripheral viewpoint, be sure to pick a character who can observe enough of the crucial events. In the photographer you have a person with the perfect right to be there and an excuse to stare. Through her viewfinder the photographer might notice the bride's red eyes, the groom's tight-lipped smile. She is free to speculate about the reasons for this, though she probably doesn't know much more about the unhappy couple than their names and how many shots they want taken before, during, and after the ceremony. However, she may have photographed enough ceremonies to have gained great insight into marriage or at least into weddings. This depth of experience may have turned her into Ann Landers, all advice and sympathy, or into an acerbic critic, the Siskel and Ebert of matrimony, voting thumbs up or down on each ceremony she photographs. Or she may be new at her job, nervous lest this one end as badly as her last stint as a topless dancer.

In Kathryn Harrison's novel *Exposure*, the point-of-view character videotapes weddings for a living. She is also a shoplifter, a diabetic who uses cocaine and may be going blind, and the only daughter of a famous photographer, now deceased, whose fast-approaching retrospective show will include nude photographs of her as a child. This list gives you a hint of the other problem, besides access to events, with a peripheral point of view. The photographer is, after all, a person, not a mere camera. The very nature of point of view means that even an outsider, one who is telling events seemingly removed from her life, becomes the human center of the readers' interest and concern. So once again your choice of viewpoint has direct consequences for the story structure. The photographer, her past and her life, can easily hijack your story. The secret is to allow your peripheral point-of-view character to be affected by the events she observes without letting the wedding deteriorate into a floral backdrop with organ music for her own story.

In a first draft, you might well discover that your story is about the photographer. As in Harrison's *Exposure*, the wedding with the tipsy grandma would be just one of several your photographer has to attend. The real heart of the story would be what is going on in her own life and marriage. This might be the happiest of discoveries, but then the photographer, not an outsider in her own life, would no longer be giving us a peripheral point of view.

Bride and Groom

Why tell the story from the periphery when you can tell it from the center, from the bride or the groom's point of view? After all, this is her wedding, his wedding. Therein lies the problem. If you choose her viewpoint, it will be her story. If you choose his, his story. If you limit yourself to one point-of-view character, you have taken sides. This choice has major consequences for the structure of the tale. Even though it's the same wedding, the groom might be ecstatic (now I'll inherit her dad's millions!) and the bride despondent (he doesn't really love me, the creep).

Maybe the bride is the perfect choice. If we are in her head and she barely thinks about the groom even as he is constantly kissing her, putting his arms around her, and telling everyone she is the light of his life, we have enough tension for any story. Or maybe the bride is the perfect one to tell the story because the guests at the wedding are almost all relatives from her colorfully odd, extended family. From her perspective, we have access to her memories, to her insider's knowledge of who is who and which cousin has been married seven times, always to women named Denise.

One way to tell a story from the bride's viewpoint and not leave the groom out is to have him occupy a central place in her thoughts. This is the approach Joy Williams takes in "Building." From the first line, "Remodeling their house is Peter's idea, Katherine likes it the way it is," the short story manages to show clearly how a husband and wife differ in their feelings about their house, about each other, and about life, even though it is from the wife's point of view.

> "I want to lose an argument with you every so often," he says, "that way the house will be more the way we both want it."
>
> But Katherine doesn't have arguments with Peter, Peter never argues with anyone. All their friends are amazed, for example, at how well he gets along with the workmen involved in the remodeling. . . . Whereas Katherine finds it difficult to converse with any of these people. Her jaws ache from projecting the illusion of concern.

Misperceptions create tension and move a story forward. Perhaps the bride wants to live in Manhattan, the groom on a farm. In a well-written short story or novel, it's important to keep the misconceptions subtle. In Robley Wilson Jr.'s short story "Wasps," the insects in the title show the difference between the point-of-view character and the younger man she is living with.

> She noticed the wasp nest on a Saturday afternoon in late July when she was mowing the lawn. It was at the east end of the house, high up under the overhang where the two roof surfaces met at the ridgepole, and it didn't amount to much yet—just a gray-celled beginning to the nest, perhaps no more than three or four inches across. The wasps were busy at it, like fervent homemakers, all their dangerous, poisonous temperament set aside for domestic preoccupations.

She wants the nest taken down, but the younger man isn't enthusiastic. Standing on the lawn she has just mowed, outside the house she owns, he shrugs and says,

> "I think we should just wait until winter, when it's so cold they can't function. Then we can knock the nest down and burn it."

By then we know this is a relationship in trouble, the kind of trouble that makes stories.

Maybe for our story, the groom's viewpoint is the best choice. Perhaps he is an outsider, meeting all his bride's strange, too closely knit family at once. This would mean he sees everything for the first time just like the readers. Or maybe he is the perfect choice because the rest of his life is a mess, and he needs just one thing to work, this wedding, this marriage, in order for his luck to change. The beginning lines of the Raymond Carver short story "Are These Actual Miles?" (mentioned in the last chapter as an example of an Into the Pot, Already Boiling opening) are from the husband's point of view, and they briskly establish both partners in the marriage and their situation.

> Fact is the car needs to be sold in a hurry, and Leo sends Toni out to do it. Toni is smart and has personality. She used to sell children's encyclopedias door to door. She signed him up, even though he didn't have kids. Afterward, Leo asked her for a date, and the date led to this. This deal has to be cash, and it has to be done tonight.

As usual in Carver's down-and-out world, his point-of-view character, Leo, is desperate, but through Leo's eyes we see that Toni is even more so in her own way.

If a given story is clearly hers or clearly his, it will be easy to choose whose eyes, ears, memories, and mind you will use. But on a day that so obviously belongs to two people, a single point of view, no matter how carefully done, that chooses the bride or the groom may always seem to leave someone out.

Multiple Viewpoints

So what do you do if no single person at the wedding can tell your story? The answer may be multiple points of view. If it is the bride's and the groom's story, why not tell it from both their perspectives? This is much like an omniscient view, such as the one used by Shirley Ann Grau in "Fever Flower," but minus the full authorial voice, the one licensed to dispense truths. Multiple viewpoints are usually handled structurally by alternation. The characters take turns.

In a novel, the point of view often alternates by chapter or by larger sections of several chapters. It may shift back and forth, rather like the ball does from player to player in tennis, or only change once, from the bride to the groom or vice versa. Chapters or sections are sometimes titled or subtitled with the point-of-view character's name.

In *As I Lay Dying*, William Faulkner uses this technique with great skill to guide readers through a novel with multiple points of view. But there doesn't have to be a fence between viewpoints. It is possible to hand off point of view like a baton in a relay race. In his novel *Madame Bovary*, nineteenth-century French novelist Gustave Flaubert handles such a transition with the simple passing of an object from one character to the other.

In a short story, often the two points of view are merely separated by a little extra white space to indicate when the change occurs, although subtitles with the characters' names are occasionally used.

In some stories, the viewpoint may simply change with the start of a new paragraph. Assume we have been in the bride's head, moving from action and dialogue down though the layers of her consciousness and back out. To change to the groom's perspective, you need only start the new paragraph with his name or the pronoun *he*, then go into his thoughts. This will signal the change (indicated here with italics).

> She wondered if she would ever be happy. "Is it time to go?" she asked.
>
> *"Almost," he said. He could see she had been crying. Why? he wondered. Was she really so unhappy with him?*

You want to be careful not to give your readers false signals, appearing to change points of view when you're not. This is an easy mistake to make, especially in a short story or novel that has already established that it has multiple points of view. It can happen after a character speaks.

> She watched as her husband-to-be paced back and forth on the edge of the platform. "I can't believe you mean that," he said. He leaned forward, looking once more down the track *but could not see the train.*

In that italicized half-sentence, the story appears to change viewpoint, to slip into the groom's head. If you mean to stay in the bride's mind, you may need to go out of your way to make this clear, substituting a line such as this:

> She saw him lean forward and look down the track, though the train was nowhere in sight.

One inevitable effect of telling the story from this double perspective is that readers will naturally compare the bride's and groom's versions of the wedding and each other; a story told by a couple almost always concerns how well or how little they know each other. One member of the couple may think the only thing good that happened on their wedding day was that the Steelers won, the other, that it was the most romantic day of their lives. (This is less of a cliché if the bride is the Steelers fan.)

There is no law limiting the number of point-of-view characters to two, though this kind of multiple point of view is more common in novels than in short stories. These authors tend to stick to two or three point-of-view characters because the more a story has the more complicated it is likely to become. Since any of these characters is always in danger of running away with the story, choosing a grandmother, a younger sister, a photographer, a dog, a bride, and a groom is a bit like driving a twenty-mule team through an obstacle course. This is not to say it cannot be done. The secret is having a central focus, such as the wedding, that is present in all the characters' thoughts. This helps unify the narrative structure.

Willa Cather does this beautifully in her short story "Neighbour Rosicky." The viewpoint shifts back and forth between Rosicky, an immigrant Nebraska farmer, the doctor who diagnoses Rosicky's bad heart, Rosicky's wife Mary, and his daughter-in-law Polly. The short story coheres because the central focus is Rosicky, and each of the characters, Rosicky included, is forced by the knowledge of the old farmer's ill health into an assessment of his life. He isn't as wealthy as his neighbors, but does that mean his life was a failure? In the end, after his patient dies, the doctor provides the final answer. He visits Rosicky's farm to see his grave and is struck by the family graveyard's beauty, which he sees as

> open and free, this little square of long grass which the wind
> for ever stirred. Nothing but the sky overhead, and the many-
> coloured fields running on until they met that sky. . . . Nothing
> could be more undeathlike than this place; nothing could be
> more right for a man who had helped to do the work of great
> cities and had always longed for the open country and had got
> to it at last. Rosicky's life seemed to him complete and beautiful.

Willa Cather's story is a model of what a multiple point-of-view short story can and should be.

The use of multiple points of view has long been a staple of the traditional novel. In novels such as *Bleak House*, Charles Dickens uses multiple perspectives to keep his many intertwined plots moving forward. He uses one character to reveal information to readers that another character does not possess. Today mystery writers like P.D. James often use the technique to withhold information, not only from another character, but from readers, using it to give just enough information to advance the plot while withholding any tidbits that would solve the mystery prematurely. Mystery writers do this by carefully choosing the viewpoint of the character who sees just enough but not too much.

If you were to use this mystery- or plot-driven model of multiple points of view for our wedding, you might choose to shift among the viewpoints of various family members and guests, all of whom might see the bride crying and speculate on the reason, until we finally arrive at the person who knows the secret of why she is weeping on her wedding day. This could be the bride, the groom, or even the suspiciously attentive hired photographer. If you take "Neighbour Rosicky" as your model, then your shifts in perspective from tipsy grandmother to kid sister to preternaturally wise wedding photographer are more to gain background information about the couple and achieve a sense of the importance of this event in their lives and the lives of their guests than to gain access to any one hidden secret. But using multiple viewpoints to control when in the story readers gain certain information would still be essentially the same as in a mystery.

A QUICK CHECKLIST

Learning about point of view by reading a book can seem like learning to play a card game by reading the rules in *Hoyle*. Relax. As you use different viewpoints in the fiction you write and notice how point of view works in the fiction you read, it will become as natural to you as poker to a professional gambler. Before we go on to the next chapter, which covers first- and second-person points of view, here's a quick review of the three basic types of third person.

1. Third-Person Omniscient Point of View. This is the all-knowing author with the ability to go into any and all characters' minds, complete freedom in time and space, and a separate authorial voice that can tell readers truths, both large and small. The strong authorial voice can provide a sense of structural unity.

2. Objective Point of View. This is the author as camera and tape recorder. The author's voice is limited to description and simple narration. The only other tool available to tell the story is dialogue. There is no access to any of the characters' minds. The strict limitations of this approach help unify the story structure.

3. Limited Omniscient Point of View. The term usually refers to a point of view that includes a purely descriptive authorial voice and access to the mind of one character (single point of view) or more (multiple points of view). Once you have set your limits, staying within them unifies the story structure.

EXERCISES

1. Write a description of your town as if seen by God. Give at least one fact from its history, some physical description of the geography, and a survey of the people who live there. Then zoom down from heaven and, as an omniscient author, describe a single house or apartment and its inhabitants. Remember, an omniscient author knows everything.

2. Now keep going. Write a short scene between two people in the house from an entirely objective point of view. Remember to limit yourself to objective description and dialogue. Then at the end of the scene, enter one of the character's minds, at least briefly, and tell us his thoughts about what just took place.

3. Keep going with this scene. Go deeper into your point-of-view character's mind, down through all the layers of consciousness. Then come back out and end the scene with dialogue or action.

4. Now stay with the same characters and situation but switch viewpoints. What is the other character thinking about the scene?

5. Rewrite some or all of the above scenes from an unconventional point of view—animal, vegetable, mineral. Compare it to the sections you wrote from a limited omniscient human perspective. Which works better?

6. Try exercises two, three, and four with more characters in the room.

7. Decide which of these different points of view worked the best. Rewrite the whole piece using that viewpoint.

CHAPTER FOUR

FIRST- AND SECOND-PERSON POINTS OF VIEW

After third person the most common point of view is first person. When we tell a story to a friend or lover or stranger on a bus, we tell it in first person. "I went to the oddest wedding on Saturday," I might say to my sister, and off into the story I would go. Or I might write her a letter that began the same way. This similarity to our everyday communications makes this viewpoint the choice of most beginning writers. Immediacy, the sense that someone is speaking directly to us, gives first person a grip on readers. How can we walk away when someone is talking to us; how can we not listen? Having someone literally tell a story gives it a natural structure. But the seeming naturalness of this approach can be deceptive. It is not easy to use well, nor is it always the best choice for telling a story.

First-person point of view has grown in popularity in this century, following that same arc I talked about earlier, from king to common man, from he and his to me and mine. Its strength, the sound of someone talking to you, is also its weakness. In the real world when a stranger, roommate, or sister starts to tell us a story, we listen critically. We judge what the person says. Were there really a *million* people waiting in line? we wonder after hearing our roommate say so, and we judge her for saying it: *She's always so dramatic. I can't quite trust what she says.* In fiction, we treat first-person narrators the same way.

In third person we are inside a character's head, privy to thoughts she would never share with anyone. We may doubt the bride's superficial judgments (she thinks hot pink is the perfect color for the groom's tuxedo), but if we are deep in her mind when she remembers her mother hitting her with a chair for not using her fork to eat her peas, it comes across as shocking and true because the presumption is that we are too far behind her defenses for her to lie. However, if a narrator tells this same story in first person, we have to decide what her reasons are for telling it before we can be sure she is not lying or exaggerating or playing on our sympathies. You cannot assume readers will automatically believe everything your first-person narrator tells them. You have to allow for this either by taking extra care to establish the narrator's trustworthiness or by turning her untrustworthiness to your narrative advantage.

THE UNRELIABLE NARRATOR

The term *unreliable narrator* is usually used to describe a particular type of untrustworthy first-person voice. Classically it is used to describe someone who is seriously out of touch with reality. Listen to the speaker in this next piece from a nineteenth-century Russian short story by Nikolai Gogol.

> So I'm in Spain. It all happened so quickly that I hardly had time to realize it. This morning the Spanish delegation finally arrived for me and we all got into the carriage. I was somewhat bewildered by the extraordinary speed at which we traveled. We went so fast that in half an hour we reached the Spanish border. But then, nowadays there are railroads all over Europe and the ships go so fast too. Spain is a strange country. When we entered the first room, I saw a multitude of people with shaven heads. I soon realized, though, that these must be Dominican or Capuchin monks because they always shave their heads. I also thought that the manners of the King's Chancellor, who was leading me by the hand, were rather strange. He pushed me into a small room and said: "You sit quiet and don't you call yourself King Ferdinand again or I'll beat the nonsense out of your head." But I knew that I was just being tested and refused to submit.

It probably did not take you long to guess the narrator is insane, and it would have taken less time if I had told you that this excerpt comes from a story called "Diary of a Madman." Because there is no separate authorial voice in first person, Gogol cannot tell us directly that his narrator is mad (except in the title). You were able to guess his condition because Gogol clearly signals us that this person's perceptions are not to be taken at face value. Even today Spain is not half an hour from any part of Russia, and it does not seem convincing when the narrator quickly decides that the multitude of the people with shaved heads are all monks. In case these more subtle clues slipped by us, Gogol throws in a clincher, the lines the "King's Chancellor" speaks.

No doubt the narrator of "Diary of a Madman" is unreliable, but it is more helpful to realize that all first-person narrators are unreliable. This is no insult. It simply means that the author signals the readers, as Gogol does, how much to believe of the story. The author who uses first-person point of view in a short story or novel can be thought of as a puppeteer. The character telling the story is the sock puppet in the author's hand. On the surface the puppet seems to be in charge of reporting events, but the author keeps peeking out from behind the curtain, winking and nodding at the audience, using dialogue and action to signal, *See how crazy he is?* It is the author who is really in charge.

Of course some narrators may be close to completely reliable. They may see the world clearly and be intelligent, humane, and likable, but when it comes to themselves or those close to them, they may be blind on some point, and therefore, in this context, unreliable. Fiction makes good use of these kinds of blind spots; for example, a plot may hinge on a husband's inability to see that his wife no longer loves him. The contrast between what the author allows us to see and what the narrator believes creates narrative tension. We read on as eager to know whether the character telling the story ever realizes how wrong he is as we are to find out if the wife actually packs up and leaves.

WHEN THE NARRATOR IS YOU

One particularly discomforting problem in first person occurs when this separation between author as puppet master and narrator as puppet collapses. This often becomes a problem when you set out to write a story with a speaker who is too much like you. It can be hard to know what will strike readers as likable or not likable, trustworthy or not, in a character who is so close to the author. I found this out when I sent an early version of an autobiographical short story to an editor who had always been kind to my work. The story was about a family car trip, and Julie, my stand-in, was the ten-year-old first-person narrator. The editor wrote back, *"Definitely not for me. Can you imagine spending three days in a car with this little girl?"* Ouch. When I reread the story, I realized that because the little girl was me, I knew her too well and hadn't bothered to find ways to characterize her that would interest adult readers. I had to gain enough distance from Julie to be able to wink at the audience when she was being a tiresome, overtalkative ten-year-old. My revised story received a much kinder note, an acceptance, on its next venture out.

Another example of the problems of writing too close to home in first person came up in a workshop I attended as a graduate student. A fellow student was writing a novel about a man who was impotent, and the impotent man in the novel was writing a novel about a man who was impotent, who was . . . I think you get the point. No doubt some members of the class weren't too interested in reading about these sexual problems, but we had a more serious problem criticizing the work than that. The fictional novelist, who was described as having the same haircut and wearing the same brand of sandals as the author, was writing a novel that was just brilliant. All the characters in the novel who read it called it a work of genius. No one in my class was willing to say that about the novel-in-progress we were reading. It was hard, given the twin identities of the writer and speaker, to assume the latter was purposefully unreliable, that he was lying about the critical response to his novel, and that the author was signalling us that he, too, knew the narrator was no Hemingway.

CHOOSING YOUR NARRATOR

First-person point-of-view characters are called *narrators* because they tell or narrate their stories. So the most basic requirement for them is that they be able and willing to tell their stories. This means they cannot be pathologically shy or monosyllabic by nature. In other words, the cat can't have their tongues. If they are normally terse, something has to have happened to shake them up and make them talk.

I am using *tell* in a loose sense here. Some of these stories seem written rather than told. In literature texts first-person narrators are often divided into two opposing camps, those that use a written or formal voice and those that use a spoken or informal voice. In practice most narrators fall in between, somewhere on a scale running from colloquial to formal, from street talk to junior Henry James. Either way there is no need to make this distinction overtly in the story. Even though your character sounds like he is talking, he doesn't need to dictate into a tape recorder or recite his account to a judge or a psychiatrist. Sometimes a story is addressed to some specific other, "If you were here, Dad, I'd tell you to your face what a shit you were." But your narrator can just start his tale, "When I was little, I believed in my father, God, and magic," and he doesn't need to be telling it to anyone but his readers, and they don't need to be directly addressed.

If your narrator sounds like he is writing his story, the same premise holds true. Though there is a grand tradition of epistolary novels, in which the story is told through letters (eighteenth-century English author Fanny Burney's *Evelina*, for example), in this century a diary or letters seem awkward and unnecessary to explain why a story sounds written. You can just do it. But as always there are exceptions.

Joyce Carol Oates' "How I Contemplated the World From the Detroit House of Correction and Began My Life Over Again" has the even longer subtitle "Notes for an Essay for an English Class at Baldwin Country Day School; Poking Around in Debris; Disgust and Curiosity; A Revelation of the Meaning of Life; A Happy Ending . . ." This short story takes its structure from the conceit that the narrator is really ordering her thoughts for a school essay about her fall from a boring middle-class existence into a world of prostitution and drugs. The short story itself has section headings that mimic an outline: "I. Events" and "II. Characters." More recently, Nick Bantock's *Griffin and Sabine*, an epistolary novel complete with envelopes, was a surprise hit.

Let's go back through the list of possible point-of-view characters for the wedding tale we used in the previous chapter and consider which might work as first-person narrators. At the bottom of each section where it applies, I'll recap the advantages of using first person or third person in that situation.

God

There is no first-person omniscient point of view. If the author is a first-person narrator, he plays a part in the story, subject to the same limitations as any other character. In experimental author Gilbert Sorrentino's *Mulligan Stew*, the author's characters conspire to take over his novel. Stories like these fall into the category of *metafiction*, fiction that calls attention to the artificial nature of fiction. God, too, occasionally appears as a first-person narrator, but since the nature of God is to be all-powerful and unknowable, giving him a role that is affected by events in the story diminishes him, making him more of a little *g* god, more just plain human. This is done in modern literature usually for comic effect (remember the *Oh, God!* movies).

Camera

There isn't such a thing as a first-person objective point of view. If we went to the trouble to give our camera a voice, "I got pointed at the bride, and I couldn't help but notice her lenses—*eyes*, humans call them—were all wet. I guess she'd been crying," then the camera is a character, and we are over in dog, horse, and pet rock as point of view territory.

Often I read stories that seem to have mistaken a first-person human narrator for a camera. In these the bride might tell us about the wedding like this.

> When I got to the church, the door was locked. I went to the side door. It was open. I went inside and turned on the light. No one was there.

It is as if she were a robot, never letting us know what she thinks or feels. It's okay for her to be repressed, slow to admit pain or pleasure, but eventually she has to let readers see the pain or pleasure breaking out from under the denial. If a character seems less like a human being and more like a video camera that just happens to be strapped to someone's head, the story is bound to read like a first draft in search of revision and some depth of characterization.

Grandma

Grandma is a good candidate for a narrator, if she's a good talker. Maybe Grandma is in a wheelchair. Telling the tale is a kind of action, and so first person is the perfect choice for a character who otherwise might seem passive. Even if she is both healthy and active, her age and experiences in life allow you to give her a voice with range, old slang to new, Yiddish to Latin, gardening metaphors to computer lingo. The trick with any first-person point of view is to introduce the voice convincingly, establish its range in the first paragraph or two, and then keep it consistent. This voice is what holds together the story and unifies the structure. Nobody does this better than Tillie Olsen in her well-known short story "I Stand Here Ironing." A social worker or teacher has asked the narrator to talk about her daughter, described as a "youngster who needs help." Here's the reply.

> I stand here ironing, and what you asked me moves tormented back and forth with the iron. . . .
> Even if I came, what good would it do? You think because I am her mother I have a key, or that in some way you could use me as a key? She has lived for nineteen years. There is all that life that has happened outside me, beyond me.

But she does go on to tell the story of her daughter's life and, bound up with it, the events of her own life, tell it in this wonderful voice whose every sentence characterizes the narrator, showing us who she is more effectively than pages of authorial description.

- If you use first person, you gain the action of having the character tell the story, an important benefit if she is otherwise inactive.
- If she is shy, secretive, or if her reliability is a problem, third person is the better choice.

Little Sister

If you choose a young narrator, just as with a young third-person point-of-view character, you gain a fresh set of eyes with which to see the world. The young often feel more intensely the wrongs and rights, the beauties and horrors of everyday life. But age becomes all-important here because young narrators have to tell their stories in their own words. It is hard to imagine a six-year-old with sufficient vocabulary and understanding to narrate any fiction capable of holding adult interest. Nine is possible, ten better, and every additional year helps. There are two ways around this central problem. One, make the kid smart. This is the central appeal of Holden Caulfield, the narrator of J.D. Salinger's classic coming-of-age novel, *The Catcher in the Rye*. He not only thinks he is smarter than the adults he meets, he is. He is also old enough to be in prep school. For a good example of how to use brainpower to enliven an even younger narrative voice, read Southern novelist Padgett Powell's book *Edisto*. Twelve-year-old Simons is skipping school and in search of a Coke in the drugstore when his mother, whom he calls the Doctor, sees him.

> She calls me over and introduces me to this gray-headed gent she's with. Now this is what gets me. She says to him, who turns out to be a barrister working land in Hilton Head, she says, "I want you to meet my protégé."
> She never includes the detail I'm her son, so I put my name into the dialogue so she might have to mention the relationship. "Simons Everson Manigault," I say to him, stepping up and pumping him a three-pump country shake, squeezing harder than even the old man said to. You say it "Simmons." I'm a rare one-*m* Simons.

Notice how quickly Powell stakes out his territory, making clear that this is a kid who can use everything from deep-South slang to words you'd think he'd have to look up. This range of vocabulary is explained in the early pages of the novel. His mother, a college professor, makes him read all her books while otherwise letting him run wild in the small North Carolina town of the title, but the explanation isn't as important as the fact that the voice works. It's compelling and varied enough to carry the story, and hidden within it is the central tension of the book. Just because a twelve-year-old boy can use big words and bad words alike doesn't mean he's an adult. We worry about Simons, rightly as it turns out.

The second way out of the young-narrator trap is to start the story in the present in an adult voice, then slip into the past using a less mature voice and world view to describe childhood times. Sometimes in a short story or novel told this way, the adult voice is present only at the beginning, but it can also form a frame that closes as well as opens the tale. Sometimes it is present at crucial junctions along the way, stepping in to interpret the younger self's perceptions. This structure allows you to have your cake and eat it too. Whole stretches can essentially recreate the consciousness of a youthful narrator while the presence of the adult voice allows for a larger vocabulary and lets you call on grown-up knowledge and reflection when needed.

This dual adult/young voice is possible because every first-person story told in past tense (the usual tense in fiction) is told as a reflection on past events and is related from somewhere beyond the end of the story. Often the presumption is that the events have just ended, and the narrator is standing, balancing as it were, on a small ledge at the end of the story, looking back. If the wedding took place on Sunday, then the narrator remembers it from the vantage point of Monday or even late Sunday night. Often this is not stated, but simply implied.

In a mixed adult/young-narrator story, the younger sister could recall the events of the wedding, which took place the summer she turned fourteen, from the distance of years, even decades. That gives you a wide range both of vocabulary and of perception. Pulitzer prize-winning novelist Richard Ford's *Wildlife* is a good example of this type of first-person narration. It begins,

> In the fall of 1960, when I was sixteen and my father was for a time not working, my mother met a man named Warren Miller and fell in love with him. This was in Great Falls, Montana, at the time of the Gypsy Basin oil boom, and my father had brought us there in the spring of that year from Lewiston, Idaho, in the belief that people—small people like him—were making money in Montana or soon would be, and he wanted a piece of that good luck before all of it collapsed and was gone in the wind.

Here we sense the distance between the speaker and his sixteen-year-old self. He sounds like a man looking back on the past, and this is enough to establish an adult voice. Only rarely do narrators come right out and give us their current ages as adults, although if one is very old or ill and being forced by time or circumstance to examine his life the way Rosicky does in Cather's story, this should be stated or implied. Sometimes at the end of a short story or novel, there are more hints about how much time has passed since the events took place. At the conclusion of *Wildlife*, the narrator's parents, separated for a while after the wrenching events of the novel, are living together again, and there is another hint that much time has passed since the events in the short story and the telling of them.

> That is how our life resumed after then, for the little time that I was at home. And for many years after that. They lived

together—that was their life—and alone. Though God knows there is still much to it that I myself, their only son, cannot fully claim to understand.

An additional benefit of this ending is that it makes clear that the events of the story had lasting consequences for both the narrator and his parents.

Another excellent example of this same technique is Stephanie Vaughn's "Able, Baker, Charlie, Dog." It opens with a line that implies a grown-up is looking back, "When I was twelve years old, my father was tall and awesome." From this one line, it is clear that the story is told at some distance by an adult narrator of unspecified age, neither very young nor very old, and that is usually enough information to satisfy readers.

- In first person you can bridge the gap between a young narrator's perceptions and your readers' adult interests by having her tell the story retrospectively from a distance of years or by making her smart.
- In third person you can use authorial voice and interpretation to help bridge the gap. This is probably the best choice for a character who is very young.

An Animal

First-person narrators need not, of course, be human. English author Anna Sewell's famous animal rights tract and children's novel, *Black Beauty*, is subtitled *The Autobiography of a Horse* and is told entirely in first person from Black Beauty's point of view.

> While I was young I lived upon my mother's milk, as I could not eat grass. In the daytime I ran by her side, and at night I lay down close by her. When it was hot, we used to stand by the pond in the shade of the trees, and when it was cold, we had a nice warm shed near the plantation.
>
> As soon as I was old enough to eat grass, my mother used to go out to work in the daytime, and come back in the evening.

Once you've made your mind up to tell the life story of a horse, there is no sense in being shy about it. Black Beauty has no trouble telling his own story or understanding the stories he overhears humans tell, as in this case of the older groom John Manly telling the story of his life to the younger James.

> . . . my father and mother died of the fever, within ten days of each other, and left me and my crippled sister Nelly alone in the world, without a relation that we could look to for help. I was a farmer's boy, not earning enough to keep myself, much less the both of us, and she must have gone to the workhouse but for our mistress (Nelly calls her her angel, and she has good right to do so).

It may strike a critical reader that in Black Beauty's world a suspiciously high number of heart-to-heart talks like that take place between humans who just happen to be in the stables, the one building where the horse can overhear them, but by convention, animal narrators are often favored by such luck.

As with first-person narrations from God's point of view, a non-human first-person point of view tends to be chosen either for comic or philosophical reasons. Comedy might be the easiest choice, but in his graphic novel *Maus*, cartoonist Art Spiegelman puts thoughts and words into the minds and mouths of mice and succeeds in conveying the horrors of the Holocaust as few other works of fiction have. When Anna Sewell published *Black Beauty* in 1877, she was out to improve the conditions of horses in England as much as or more than to entertain. Is there a larger philosophical point to be made about the life of Seeing Eye dogs that would justify using one for our narrator?

- In first person you have the additional burden of making the reader believe the animal narrator is not only aware of the meaning of events, but capable of telling its own story. This makes the character more anthropomorphic, more human, than that same animal would be in third-person point of view.
- In third person the presumption is that the author is acting as interpreter for the wordless animal. This makes it a slightly more believable point of view.

Photographer

Peripheral point-of-view characters in the first person are called *peripheral narrators*. The classic example is Nick Carraway in F. Scott

Fitzgerald's *The Great Gatsby*. The novel is the story of Gatsby's life as the title suggests, but Gatsby has too many secrets and guards them too carefully to make a good first-person narrator. He literally would not tell his own story. But Nick is not just a video camera, a set of eyes and ears; his attraction to Gatsby and his choosing to tell the story show how deeply his brief involvement with the bootlegger affected him. In many ways the novel is not the story of Gatsby, but of Nick. Just as with peripheral point-of-view characters, remember that no matter how far outside the action a narrator is, what happens has to affect him as well as those he observes. If the photographer is our first-person narrator, this wedding, more than all others, has to change or at least threaten to change what she thinks about marriage, weddings, or life.

- The first-person peripheral narrator has two advantages. Although not involved in the main action, his telling the story gives him an active role, something to do. Also, telling the story gives him ample opportunity to reveal how he was affected by the events he observed.
- Third person may be the better choice if you want to have free and reliable access to all levels of your peripheral point-of-view character's mind.

Bride and Groom

It is possible to tell a story from both the bride's and the groom's first-person points of view, though having two narrators competing for attention can make a story seem like a long session at a marriage counselor's office. Structurally, if the short story is divided in halves or thirds (bride-then-groom or groom-bride-groom) or if the novel is divided by chapters or larger sections, it helps to avoid the feeling that each narrator is waiting for the next sentence or paragraph to elbow the other out of the way. Jane Hamilton's novel *A Map of the World* is divided into three sections. The first and concluding sections are from Alice's point of view. The middle, from her husband Howard's. The novel opens with the accidental drowning of a neighbor's child in Alice and Howard's pond while Alice is baby-sitting the girl. The accident leaves Alice prostrate with grief and guilt. Howard, whom Alice sees as the calm, competent one, demands she get on with life.

"Alice," he said, sitting down beside my head, "it's time to get up." He didn't sound angry. He wasn't shouting. He was never one to pick a fight; if someone asked him, I'm sure he would say we had never had a cross word in our life together. He was looking at me dispassionately, I thought, the way he might watch a middle-aged bank clerk count his deposit.

But after Alice is arrested, charged with sexually abusing children at the school where she works part-time as a nurse, Howard is anything but calm.

Alice has sometimes told people, I guess in a way I find objectionable, as if I'm a show animal, that one of my strong points is my ability to stay calm. She had been excessively calm on the telephone, all things considered. I already felt the need to make up somehow for what she had lacked. I careened from the paper-towel dispenser to the refrigerator to the cupboard. I went around the room a couple of times trying to make something other than Marshmallow Fluff sandwiches for my daughters.

Alice doesn't know how to tell Howard about the grief she feels over her part in the drowning. Howard doesn't *really* know whether Alice is capable of hurting a child on purpose. In this case the two points of view are used to underscore the sad truth that we can never truly know other people, no matter how much time we spend with them or how much we love them. That may be the theme of any short story or novel that invites readers to compare lovers' thoughts.

Remember that with any multiple point of view, this structure inevitably means you are going to have to pick one of the characters to be your final point of view. Jane Hamilton chooses to start and finish with Alice. If you try to make flying return visits to each narrator's head in order to conclude the story, you will end up with airsick and confused readers, and you will still be in one character's head last anyway. Ideally, in terms of structure, the closing narrator or point-of-view character should be someone who can act or observe an action that will clearly close the story for all the point-of-view characters.

- Dual point of view in first person runs the risk of seeming as if there are too many narrators telling the same story, too many people talking, but if both characters have distinct and interesting voices, it is a risk worth taking.

- Dual point of view is more common and natural in third person since the omniscient or limited omniscient author can move easily between the two characters. In either first or third person, it can be used to conceal information from readers to help advance the plot.

Multiple Narrators

A story in which everyone at the wedding takes turns as narrator risks sounding more like trial transcript with each character taking turns testifying. It can be hard structurally to separate so many voices in such a small space, but it is possible. In *As I Lay Dying*, William Faulkner uses a host of narrative voices. Some family members and outsiders reappear at intervals in the book. Others have only a single chapter to tell us their versions of events. This is true of the dead mother who tells her story, the linchpin of the book, in a mere eight pages. A wedding, an event of communal significance like a funeral, might be the ideal setting for a story told by a host of narrators.

- First-person multiple point of view is used when it suits the complicated nature of the story to have a host of sometimes conflicting, sometimes agreeing voices. The danger is that it can get cacophonous.

- Third-person multiple point of view is more common in novels than in short stories. Authorial voice is often used to tie the characters and the story together. In short stories, having all the point-of-view characters thinking about a single person or problem can work the same way.

Another strategy for telling the story of an event of great importance to a group is *collective narration*. Faulkner uses this technique in his short story "A Rose for Emily." *I* is never used in the story. It is always *we*, even in the story's closing paragraph, when, after Miss Emily's death, the townspeople find the corpse of her dead lover laid out on a bed in a locked room in her house.

Then we noticed that in the second pillow was the indentation of a head. One of us lifted something from it, and leaning

forward, that faint and invisible dust dry and acrid in the nos-
trils, we saw a long strand of iron-gray hair.

The collective voice heightens Miss Emily's status as outside the
homogeneous body of the town and makes the people of the town
one in their actions and guilt.

- Collective point of view is rare in first person. It implies a single
  narrator within the collective because there is a single voice, but
  that narrator never identifies himself.
- Third-person collective point of view is even rarer in fiction but
  possible. It is actually an offbeat form of omniscient point of view
  in which the author goes into a set of minds at once, reporting
  only the group response: "The Biggs always got up at eight. They
  loved pancakes. They hated waffles." You could use this point of
  view to characterize a nation, a family, or a set of triplets. It is
  hard to maintain for an entire short story or novel.

SECOND-PERSON POINT OF VIEW

The least common point of view is second person. Like first person it
has grown in popularity, especially in the past twenty years, but it
remains an experimental distant cousin of those two better established
points of view, first and third. In fiction written in the third-person
point of view, the characters, when not called by name, are *he, she*, or
they. In first-person point of view, *I* or *we*. The pronoun used in second
person for the point-of-view character is always *you*, as in, *You enter
the room, look around, take a seat.*

The mere occasional appearance of the pronoun *you* does not mean
a story is in second person. An omniscient author can address readers,
for example, "So you see, dear reader, our Nell was in a terrible fix.
She sat at her dressing table, weeping, thinking of her Tom, now lost
to her forever," without changing the fact that the story is being told
from a third-person omniscient viewpoint. A first-person narrator may
address another character, such as, "You were right, Dad. I didn't
amount to much. I just turned out happy. And for you, that would
never have been enough." No matter, the story is still being told from a
first-person point of view. These direct addresses are brief, purposeful
lapses in the structure of the narration, rhetorical flourishes to drive
home a point, but they are not true second-person point of view.

In true second person, readers are converted into the character; the distance between readers and the story collapses. This is the case in Lorrie Moore's short story "Amahl and the Night Visitors: A Guide to the Tenor of Love."

> Understand that your cat is a whore and can't help you. She takes on love with the whiskery adjustments of a gold-digger. She is a gorgeous nomad, an unfriend. Recall how just last month when you got her from Bob downstairs, after Bob had become suddenly allergic, she leaped into your lap and purred, guttural as a German chanteuse, familiar and furry as a mold. And Bob, visibly heartbroken, still in the room, sneezing and giving instructions, hoping for one last cat nuzzle, descended to his hands and knees and jiggled his fingers in the shag. The cat only blinked.

The hook is immediate: "Understand that *your* cat is a whore and can't help *you*." That is the great attraction of second person: It commands your readers' attention. And it involves readers intimately and immediately in the story, since they are the character. In this way it functions as a literary form of virtual reality. There you are on the page, and you are getting a cat from a guy named Bob.

This approach has its risks as well. What if a reader puts her foot down, refuses to become a character? *I don't have a cat*, she thinks and closes the book. This resistance is one reason second person has remained marginal and is used more often for short stories than for whole novels. However, Jay McInerney's novel *Bright Lights, Big City* is written entirely in this viewpoint, and it became a best-seller, a symbol then and now of the success and excess of the Reagan-era 1980s, much as *The Great Gatsby* came to stand as the literary model of the Roaring Twenties. The novel begins this way.

> You are not the kind of guy who would be at a place like this at this time of the morning. But here you are, and you cannot say that the terrain is entirely unfamiliar, although the details are fuzzy. You are at a nightclub talking to a girl with a shaved head. The club is either Heartbreak or the Lizard Lounge.

Here second person combines with present tense to create a sense of urgency that yanks us into the book. Even as McInerney drags us into the nightspot, he cleverly admits that we're not the kind who would usually be in such a place. This helps cut our resistance. Who wouldn't want to stick around to find out more about the girl with the shaved head?

Some writers are attracted to second person because it is used so rarely. It is a point of view without the long and complicated traditions of first and third person, and its potential is largely untapped. Maybe you will be the writer to take it to new heights, to become the one whose work is always quoted in books like this.

EXERCISES

1. Write a scene in which your first-person narrator describes some simple event, such as dinner at a restaurant with a friend or shopping in a grocery store. Use a character who is much like you, with a similar vocabulary. Remember that a consistent voice is the key to structural unity in first-person point of view.

2. Now rewrite the scene and make the narrator slightly unreliable. (Perhaps she is an anorexic who sees all food in terms of danger. Perhaps she is a snob who looks down on everyone around her.)

3. Rewrite the scene a third time, but make the narrator strongly and obviously unreliable. (Maybe she thinks the food is poisoned or that people are reading her mind.)

4. Write a paragraph in first person in the most informal spoken voice that feels natural to you. Try to pretend you are on the telephone with a friend; use slang. You are not trying for parody here. Don't sound like someone your best friend wouldn't know. Just go for casual but realistic.

5. Now write the paragraph in the most formal written first-person narrative voice that feels natural. Don't try to sound like a lawyer or philosophy professor (unless you are one), but allow yourself to use that part of your vocabulary you probably don't use when grocery shopping or walking the dog but that feels comfortable to you from your reading and writing. If it helps, write it in the form of a letter or diary entry.

6. Put the two paragraphs from exercises four and five side by side. How different are they? Which is better? What are the strengths and weaknesses of each first-person voice? What kind of story would the spoken voice be best for? The written? Go back over your list of

Potential Story Ideas and mark which ones seem more suited to a spoken, casual narrative voice, which ones a more formal one.

7. Write a scene about a dance from the point of view of a narrator who is considerably older than you. Make sure she is the one dancing and that the scene reminds her in some way of her past.

8. Rewrite the dance scene from the point of view of a thirteen-year-old. A ten-year-old. A six-year-old. How far back can you go before the voice seems too young to tell the story or to hold an adult reader's interest?

9. Rewrite the scene again, making the narrator, of whatever age, a peripheral one. The narrator does not get to dance, but views the central events from some physical or emotional distance and is drawn for some reason to the story of those who do dance. As you write the scene, discover what that reason is.

10. Rewrite the same scene from an unconventional point of view: animal, vegetable, or mineral.

11. Rewrite the scene so there are at least two separate first-person points of view (ninety-year-old woman first, then six-year-old; or thirteen-year-old, then dog). What do you gain by having two narrators? What do you lose?

12. Rewrite the dance scene in second person (*As the music starts, you move onto the floor . . .*).

CHAPTER FIVE

CONSTRUCTING CHARACTERS

C haracters are people who just happen to live in stories and books. When you are writing, you bring everything you already know about the world to the blank page, and that includes what you know about human beings. Characterization is therefore an area of fiction in which you already possess well-developed skills. But though you may be renowned among your friends and colleagues as a good judge of character, may have made As in all your psychology courses, may be the person everyone turns to for sage advice, this alone will not guarantee your ability to make people come to life on the page. In the real world everybody just exists. In fiction, characters, like all structural elements, have to be carefully and painstakingly built.

Your goal is to construct ones who could be mistaken for human beings instead of robots, cartoons, or characters from other people's stories. I'll approach the issue starting on the outside, making suggestions how to build your characters using appearance, mannerisms, tastes, speech, and other traits perceived by the five senses. Then I'll consider how to furnish the inside, providing the thoughts, emotions, aspirations, and nightmares that make someone seem psychologically real. I'll also discuss some categories of character (minor, central, flat, and round) that will help you decide how much space to devote to each character depending on her function in the structure of the story. Finally I'll look at the connections between your own personality and the people you create. Throughout you will find practical tips and rules that will help you construct characters that readers will believe in.

EXTERIOR CHARACTERIZATION

Since we perceive those around us from the outside, writing external descriptions of others comes naturally. Even a point-of-view character who will later offer his childhood memories and deepest fears is often introduced with exterior description. In fiction, as in life, first impressions count. In the real world, if you meet a man at a party, you will not be able to read his mind. Yet before he says a word, you may think, I'll bet he's a lawyer (or car salesman or male model or painter) based solely on his appearance and mannerisms. You may be perfectly right. After all you have had a lifetime of meeting people on which to base this judgment.

Third-person omniscient point of view allows the author to tell this to readers directly: "The man who shook Carol's hand was a lawyer." Just as easily a third-person point-of-view character could say, "Carol could tell he was a lawyer," or your first-person narrator could remark, "I could tell right off he was a lawyer." But as I warned you in the chapters on point of view, contemporary readers have developed a considerable resistance to being told what to think, even about such minor matters as a character's profession. So if you plan to pronounce the man a lawyer or have a character or narrator do so, it's good to add corroborating details. What about his appearance and manner so clearly reveals his profession? His suit? Haircut? Tie? Shoes? The way he strides or bounds or slithers across the room? The word *lawyer* may bring up a different mental picture in readers' minds than it does in yours. The details you provide are your chance to control what they see and thus control your story. If you say the first thing Carol notices about the man is his Armani suit, you are talking about one kind of lawyer and character. If she notices his rumpled Sears sports jacket, pocket bulging with cards saying *Injured? Call 1-800-Sue-Them*, you have an entirely different animal to deal with.

One rule to remember in describing how someone looks is not to overdo it. If you say, "Carol had never before seen a red-haired man with the nerve to wear a pink plaid jacket," readers get an image they can hold onto. *Red hair*, they think, *pink coat*. If you add, "The coat was too large for such a short man and clashed with his two-tone saddle oxfords and paisley bow tie, neither of which did anything to make his watery blue eyes any clearer or the wart on his nose any less repulsive," your readers are like a juggler tossed one too many balls. *Red, green, large, small, two-tone, paisley, eyes, wart, nose, repulsive*—details get dropped and their minds go blank. Later when you refer to "the man with the wart" or "the man in the pink coat," readers will wonder, *Who?*

Charles Dickens is an acknowledged master of the art of defining a person with an opening description. Since his novels have dozens of characters, Dickens must be both efficient and effective in introducing them or his narrative would collapse into chaos. In *Bleak House* Esther Summerson, the young narrator, describes the visiting Mrs. Pardiggle this way.

> She was a formidable style of a lady, with spectacles, a prominent nose, and a loud voice, who had the effect of wanting a great deal of room. And she really did, for she knocked down little chairs with her skirts that were quite a great way off.

Dickens' description works because all the details add up, culminating with those poor little chairs, leaving us with the strong impression of a woman who takes up more space than is comfortable physically and, by extension, psychologically. He does it without overloading us. He gives just three physical details (*spectacles, nose, voice*), colors them with adjectives (*formidable, prominent, loud*), and then cements them in our memory with a delightful miniature anecdote ("she knocked down little chairs"). This is a useful technique and one that works perfectly to help readers remember the woman and her place in the novel's complicated structure.

Another example of telling details comes in Vietnam veteran Tim O'Brien's short story "The Things They Carried." Each man is introduced and defined by a list of what he hauls through the jungle.

> As a first lieutenant and platoon leader, Jimmy Cross carried a compass, maps, code books, binoculars, and a .45-caliber pistol that weighed 2.9 pounds fully loaded. He carried a strobe light and the responsibility for the lives of his men. . . .
>
> As a medic, Rat Kiley carried a canvas satchel filled with morphine and plasma and malaria tablets and surgical tape and comic books and all the things a medic must carry,

including M&Ms for especially bad wounds, for a total
weight of nearly 20 pounds.

These lists may seem to violate my earlier injunction against not
overdoing description. But these lists of belongings don't overwhelm
because readers aren't really asked to remember each item, just the
cumulative impression they leave of a character's rank and specialty.
Jimmy Cross, the leader. Rat Kiley, the medic. Without this clear
introduction to each soldier, readers could not remember who is who
as they move through a short story whose structure is that of a collective history of the unit and each man in it.

In "Powerhouse" renowned Southern writer Eudora Welty uses a
different technique for establishing a character's place in her short
story's structure. She makes Powerhouse's ever-changing appearance
the focus, taking readers along as the narrator attempts to describe a
jazzman who can't really be described.

> There's no one in the world like him. You can't tell what he
> is. . . . Asiatic, monkey, Jewish, Babylonian, Peruvian, fanatic,
> devil. He has pale gray eyes, heavy lids, maybe horny like a
> lizard's, but big glowing eyes when they're open. He has Af-
> rican feet of the greatest size, stomping, both together, on
> each side of the pedals. He's not coal black—beverage col-
> ored—he looks like a preacher when his mouth is shut, but
> then it opens—vast and obscene.

The shifting visual description serves a vital purpose, establishing
Powerhouse as a larger-than-life, nearly mythical being. Who he is
and isn't, the difficulty in defining him, is the central point of this
opening description and of the entire story.

Not only is the choice of details important in characterization, the
order in which you present them also requires thought. When we
enter a room we naturally move our gaze from near to far or left to
right. When we meet a person, we look him over, quite literally, from
head to toe. No matter how we move our gaze, there is a natural
order to our perceptions. Sometimes in fiction this order is slightly
rearranged for emphasis in the same way that a painter uses her
control to highlight a certain figure or detail.

In chapter two I told you about my decision to start my short story

"Underground Women" with a set piece. The story opens with a photographer taking a picture of a woman on the floor of a Paris laundromat and describing how the light lets her

> catch this scene, this knot of official people grouped casually
> around a dark wrinkled shape on the floor. Catch at an angle
> of extreme foreshortening the stubby, already almost blue
> legs, the one outflung hand holding one black sock.
> It will be the photograph of a dead woman.

The structure of this description follows the way the photographer sees the details as she peers through the viewfinder, her eyes moving over the fallen woman (legs first, then outflung hand, then sock) before they pull back and she takes in the meaning of what has happened, that the woman on the floor is dead. The larger perspective is deliberately delayed for effect.

Presenting details in a spatially logical order seems so simple, but mistakes can happen. In his book, *Making Shapely Fiction*, writing teacher Jerome Stern gives this example of the unintentional consequences of violating the normal order of perception: "The rat's whiskered nose, gray body, long hairless tail, and glittering red eye." Saving the eye for last has made it a science fiction rat, a single red eye bobbing on the tip of its hairless tail.

Characters Speaking

What characters look like is important, but just as useful for external characterization is how they speak. The lawyer I talked about earlier could simply reach out to shake a hand and introduce himself as "Jim Babbs, of Babbs, Lawson, and Jurgenson, Attorneys at Law." Or, more subtly, he could let slip in the midst of conversation, "Now if I'd been your divorce lawyer . . ." Dialogue is one of the great tools of fiction, one every writer uses, if to slightly different purposes. Ernest Hemingway, notoriously laconic, might have someone say in five words what a novelist like Joseph Conrad would have thought worthy of a speech running several paragraphs.

How do you know what your characters should say and how exactly they should say it? As with most things in writing, you have two basic sources for instruction and inspiration: life and literature. In fiction people speak in shorter bursts than they do in life. If you have ever listened to a politician or had a loved one go to the trouble of telling you everything he can't stand about you, you know that in print such dialogue would run for pages upon pages. In fiction a more typical exchange is like the one in Marly Swick's "The Still Point," in which the narrator visits her deadbeat Buddhist husband in jail after sending him a letter telling him their marriage is over.

> "Almost five years," I choked out. "Don't you even feel sad?" I felt as if my heart were being crushed like a walnut. He let go of me, tore open the bag of dried papaya with his teeth and offered me one, as if he were offering me some really precious gift. . . . "Bottom line," he said, popping a slice into his mouth, "life is suffering."
> "You don't know what suffering is," I told him, "until you've been married to you!"

Maybe this is simply the economy of art (painters don't usually paint every pore either), or maybe it represents what we actually remember from longer exchanges. There are variations by author and character (even in novels people tend to speak at greater length in Mississippi than in Maine), but generally conversations in fiction come to the point more quickly and are more likely to have a point than in life. If you want to make clear that the conversation did go on and on, you can imply it with summary dialogue, like this.

> "You wouldn't believe how many people don't even have a will," Jim Babbs, of Babbs, Lawson, and Jurgenson, Attorneys at Law said. Carol nodded absently, and he went on, and on and on. Going through case after case of husbands leaving wives, tiny twins, beloved aunts, or schnauzers penniless because of the lack of good legal planning.

Summary can also be used to imply the everyday nature of a conversation, a dialogue that is so much of a type it doesn't deserve a closer reporting.

> Carol had come to see George, but after a quick, "Thank God, you're here," he'd disappeared into his duties as the host, leaving her to listen to the others drone on about which movie or restaurant or play was terribly overrated and whether high tech stocks were headed up or down.

If you are uncertain about whether a line of dialogue or a whole conversation belongs in a story, there is a simple test: Every line must be both interesting and either add to your readers' understanding of your character or help establish a sense of place or advance the plot. The best dialogue works overtime to do all these things at once.

A small word of warning here about dialogue tags, those ubiquitous *he said*s and *she said*s at the end of nearly every line of dialogue. How characters speak is often as important as what they say. The ideal is to have a distinct voice for each character, so distinct that readers can tell without dialogue tags which character is talking. In reality this won't always be the case, and nothing irritates readers more than getting to the end of a line of dialogue and wondering, *Hey, who said that?* You can occasionally skip a tag in a conversation. If Betty and David are fighting, taking turns dishing it out, readers can usually figure out that the line after David's is Betty's. Skip too many and they must count back, *David, Betty, David*, climbing the page to reach the last dialogue tag to be sure who said that last particularly cutting quip. No reader will thank you for that extra burden.

Often writers, too aware of all the *said*s they've been typing, want to break the monotony and so resort to *Betty sputtered* or *David expostulated*. These nonstandard tags only call attention to themselves. For readers, *he said* or *she asked* are as invisible as punctuation. Who really notices commas, periods and question marks unless they are incorrect or missing? This is not to say you can never use a *he shouted* or *she whispered*, but a better tactic for adding variety is to include some small action accompanied by the character's name or the appropriate pronoun, placed either before or after the dialogue.

> "I just don't know." Betty bit her lip.
> David shook his head. "Yes, you do."

Similarly, be sparing when adding adverbs to dialogue tags to signal how a line is meant. If you write,

> "Go to Hell," he said, angrily.

the *angrily* is redundant because readers will naturally read a line like "Go to Hell" that way. On the other hand, if you write,

> "Go to Hell," he said, pleasantly.

the *pleasantly* comes too late to tell readers not to take *Go to Hell* as angry. Readers have to go back over the line, changing the first angry reading to something softer. Better to set up the proper reading of the line in advance.

> He smiled at his brother and punched him lightly on the arm. "Go to Hell," he said. They were more than brothers. They were best friends and always would be.

Dialect

Ideally each character's voice should be so distinct that even without dialogue tags your readers can tell who is speaking. But is it really possible to reproduce on the page the sound of spoken language? To recreate the way a wheat farmer from Grand Forks, North Dakota, sounds versus a Memphis hairdresser or a Havana cigar maker or an advertising executive from Manhattan? The answer is no, but we should make an effort anyway. In American writing there is a long tradition of using dialect to convey differences in speech due to region, class, ethnicity, and race. Writers such as Bret Harte and Mark Twain struggled to bring to the page the speech of the West, Zona Gale that of the Middle West, Joel Chandler Harris, the black dialect of the South, and Kate Chopin and George Washington Cable the distinct culture of one famous southern city, New Orleans. There were many others.

In Mark Twain's novel *Huckleberry Finn*, Huck's father, drunk and greedy, has heard that his son has come into some money. He says to Huck,

> "Looky here—mind how you talk to me; I'm a-standing about all I can stand, now—so don't gimme no sass. I've been in town two days, and I hain't heard nothing but about you bein' rich."

Notice how Twain combines regional expressions or slang and phonetic spellings (or misspellings) designed to indicate how a word is pronounced. These techniques are the basic repertoire of dialect, and writers pick and choose to convey their character's version of English. Before you choose dialect as a technique you want to use, you should be aware of how it is likely to affect both your story structure and readers' perceptions of your fiction. To do this it helps to know a bit more about the history of its use.

The tradition of using dialect in fiction is not solely an American one. Charles Dickens often uses it to convey differences in British class and region. In *The Pickwick Papers* the coachman, Samuel Weller, discusses the difficulty of identifying the source of meat in a purchased veal pie.

> "Weal pie," said Mr. Weller, soliloquizing, as he arranged the eatables on the grass. "Wery good thing is weal pie, when you know the lady as made it, and is quite sure it an't kittens; and arter all though, where's the odds, when they're so like weal that the wery pieman themselves don't know the difference?"

The effect here is undeniably comic, especially when the *weal*s and *wery*s of Weller are contrasted with the upper-class speech of the Pickwickians. Unfortunately, I have never heard this particular British accent. I hear Elmer Fudd's voice when I read Weller. This is also a comic voice, but perhaps not what Dickens intended. Also under this heading falls the tendency to leave the *g* off words ending in *ing*, as in *goin'* and *dancin'*. Both English mystery-writer Dorothy Sayers' aristocratic sleuth Lord Peter Wimsey and Mark Twain's Mississippi River folk drop the *g*, and yet one cannot suppose these characters sound much alike. These last two examples should warn you that just because you can hear the speaker's voice in your head as you write doesn't mean your readers will hear the same dialect when they read. Our alphabet and punctuation marks are not up to the exact transcription of speech.

Of course dialect, like everything else, is a matter of degree. Most readers wouldn't find Huck's father's or Sam Weller's dialect too difficult to follow. The speech of Huck's friend Jim, the slave he accompanies down the Mississippi on a raft, may be a different matter. When Huck and Tom Sawyer sneak up on him, Jim calls out,

> "Say—who is you? Whar is you? Dog my cats ef I didn' hear sumf'n. Well, I knows what I's gywne to do. I's gwyne to set down here and listen tell I hears it agin."

Here we have it all. The syntax of speech (*who is you, I hears it*) instead of the syntax of the grammar books (*who are you, I hear it*), obscure local expressions (*dog my cats*), and phonetic indications of local pronunciation (*whar, sumf'n, gwwne*). It is not a style most readers find easy to follow. For that reason alone, think long and hard before blessing a character with a dialect equally as dense. The effect is paradoxical. In its written form the most informal speech becomes nearly as hard to understand as a foreign language. As a practical matter, it often means that information conveyed by a person speaking dialect has to be repeated by the author or a character whose speech readers can more easily understand. This takes up a good bit of space and can slow down your plot.

By the 1960s other objections to this kind of dialect began to surface. African-American writers were especially vocal in their indignation at the way blacks were portrayed in the works of white writers like Joel Chandler Harris, Mark Twain, and Harriet Beecher Stowe. These portrayals were—and still are—seen as racist, though there are some young African-American writers, such as the novelist Sapphire, who use heavy dialect. Still the general trend has been away from any heavy use of phonetic spelling. Many people feel that to misspell words to show their pronunciation implies that the speakers are illiterate, that if they wrote the same words they would misspell them. Others point out the obvious: Since English does not have a consistent system of phonetic spelling, misspelling one word (*sump'n* for *something*) to make it authentic as dialect doesn't make much sense when a word like *though* might fall right next to it spelled the standard way even though it's really pronounced *tho*. And anyway, are *sez* and *stummick* really pronounced differently than *says* and *stomach*?

Writers, including African-American authors such as Toni Morrison, now generally try to show their characters' speech without resorting to phonetic misspelling. This is certainly the case in this scene from Morrison's novel *Jazz*, in which a woman working as a maid speaks about her employers.

> "Knew both of them from way back. Come up here, the whole family act like they never set eyes on me before. Comes from handling money instead of a broom which I better get to before I lose this no-count job."

This seems like a reasonable compromise between legibility and truthfulness to the dialect. All readers of English can follow the sense, and those familiar with African-American speech will add distinctive pronunciations as they read. It can be as effective and efficient as Dickens' descriptions in establishing a character in readers' minds.

If you are like me, you will want to take advantage of every possible tool to bring your characters to life, and this brings us to some often neglected details that can make the people in your writing seem real. For example speech isn't the only sound they make. They can also have squeaky shoes or a habit of whistling in the dark or of listening to Bach chorales on their CD players. Sherlock Holmes plays endless melancholy serenades on his violin. Holden Caulfield smokes and coughs his way through *The Catcher in the Rye*. Listen to the people around you on the bus or in a busy elevator. Close your eyes. You'll find that even without speaking they make all kinds of fascinating noises.

Texture, Smell, Taste

With external characterization you can also appeal to your readers' other senses by using texture, smell, and taste. You can overtly call up a sensation by saying a man is wearing a coat of *rough* wool. Or you can simply say he is wearing a tweed coat, so that even without the adjective *rough*, readers receive a different tactile sensation than if you had said he is wearing a satin smoking jacket. This is an economical way of establishing a character.

You can also have a character wear perfume or eat too much garlic. The sense of smell is closely tied to memory, and a particular scent might have deep significance. Whenever I smell pine needles I am instantly back in Girl Scout camp deep in the Ocala National Forest in Florida. This even happened to me once in a Greek restaurant where the smell of pine came from a bottle of retsina. You can imply smell by having a guest bring a bouquet of flowers to a party. The Victorians wrote entire books about the language of flowers, detailing which blossoms to include in a bouquet sent to a loved one. Even in contemporary fiction someone who brings a dozen hothouse roses to the hostess of a party is a different person from the one who brings a lilac branch hastily broken from a bush in her backyard.

Like flowers, food makes a wonderful addition to a story and can be used to effectively develop a character. A man who eats an Italian sausage sandwich for lunch is different from a diner who orders a salad of organic greens. A friend wrote a wonderful story about a beautiful divorced woman who brings a large ham, dotted with cloves and draped with rings of pineapple, to a neighbor's house after his funeral. The etiquette of food in this small town dictates that only those very close to the dear departed bring large, expensive dishes. Neighbors and acquaintances are supposed to limit themselves to desserts such as pies or side dishes such as creamed corn or home-made pickles. So by the single act of bringing the huge ham, the divorcée is telling the widow and everyone else that she had been having an affair with the dead man and that she doesn't care who knows it. In this story the divorced woman is really just a walking version of the ham, both lovely and terribly out of place. The author's method of characterization is intricately connected to her story's structure. The ham sends a message that causes the story's main conflict.

In your fiction consider having your characters touch, smell, and even taste each other. This makes them seem human and connected. A woman can find her father's hands cold or chapped, notice her mother's fingertips smell like garlic or her daughter's hair like peach shampoo, discover her lover's skin tastes salty or her husband's mouth like day-old coffee. This will help make your cast more real, keep them from seeming like paper dolls cut out by the author or ghosts who only talk, talk, talk.

INTERIOR CHARACTERIZATION

The exterior tells only part of the story. To develop truly complex and satisfying characters, we must develop interior lives for them revealing their thoughts, memories, dreams, and imaginings. Unless you have decided to restrict it severely, the point of view you choose for your story or novel commits you to develop at least one person from the inside out. When Holden Caulfield, the young narrator of J.D. Salinger's novel *The Catcher in the Rye*, visits his teacher, we probably gain as much a sense of who he is as we learn about old Spencer.

> . . . there were pills and medicine all over the place, and everything smelled like Vicks Nose Drops. . . . What made it even more depressing, old Spencer had on this very sad, ratty old bathrobe that he was probably born in or something. I don't much like to see old guys in their pajamas and bathrobes

anyway. Their bumpy old chests are always showing. And
their legs. Old guys' legs, at beaches and places, always look
so white and unhairy. "Hello, sir," I said. "I got your note.
Thanks a lot."

Although Holden's description is of one man, we get a strong sense
that he has a nearly physical revulsion to old age. It's depressing, sad,
and ratty, and only looks worse when taken outdoors in the light.
Holden's interior repulsion stands in complete contrast to his perfectly
polite actions. Without his thoughts, we would have no idea how he
really felt about Spencer or old men in general. This contrast between
exterior action and interior thought creates tension, a tension that
structurally helps to establish then advance the plot. Even though he
knows it is inevitable, Holden does not want to become like the adults
he sees around him. We read on to see where this impossible desire
will lead him.

To take us even closer to his deepest feelings about life, we need
just the right memory, dream, or vision to explain who he truly is,
who he wants to be if it is not a grown-up. Finding just the right detail
for this kind of interior characterization is always hard. For Holden it
comes when he tells his little sister, Phoebe, what he wants to do with
his life.

"Anyway, I keep picturing all these little kids playing some
game in this big field of rye and all. Thousands of little kids,
and nobody's around—nobody big, I mean—except me. And
I'm standing on the edge of some crazy cliff. What I have to
do, I have to catch everybody if they start to go over the
cliff—I mean if they're running and they don't look where
they're going I have to come out from somewhere and *catch*
them. That's all I'd do all day. I'd just be the catcher in the
rye and all."

So there it is. The young man who finds adults either revolting or
hypocritical has a fantasy in which he is *big*, but not *old*, and serves as
the tender protector of thousands of little children frolicking outdoors.

The most effective memory or thought is always the one that is
hidden, that the character is reluctant to reveal. Its revelation can
make readers forgive or at least understand someone's failings. This

is certainly true for Holden Caulfield, and it is what defense lawyers do instinctively these days when they try to find the right detail from their clients' pasts (broken homes, sexual abuse) to make their crimes seem understandable, even excusable. The lawyers could well have learned this technique from fiction writers.

This defense works because it mirrors the way we see our lives and the lives of those around us. A student of mine was writing a story I suspected was autobiographical about a woman with claustrophobia. Because other students found the character to be less than convincing, the author kept adding more and more background, trying to explain where the problems had started. She added a scene in which the young character's mother went on a business trip leaving the child's heart broken and then another in which the girl smoked pot with a boyfriend and experienced an attack of paranoia. Something still seemed lacking. Then while we were talking in my office, the student let slip that when she was three she'd been coming home with her father when he suddenly had a heart attack in the elevator of their apartment building and died. She had been too young to know how to work the elevator and was trapped alone with her father's body until someone pushed the button on another floor. On my advice she revealed late in her story that her character had just such a memory, changing the father to a mother to distance it a bit from her own experience and to make it fit better with the cast she'd already developed. No one who read the story in its revised form had any trouble understanding why the central character, even as an adult, preferred to live in a ground-floor apartment or why she had claustrophobia, yet the explanation seemed neither obvious nor trite. It felt true because it was a telling detail, well told, and because it came in the right place in the short story's structure.

MINOR, CENTRAL, FLAT, AND ROUND

When I was in literature classes in high school and college, we learned terms for different types of characters: *minor, central, flat,* and *round.* When I started writing I couldn't help wondering what if anything terms like those meant for my fiction. I imagined one of my characters as Goldilocks wandering through the three bears' house. Papa Bear's bed is too central and round, Mama Bear's bed, too minor and flat, but Baby Bear's bed is just right, so Goldilocks climbs in and soon is fast asleep. Eventually I decided there were some useful concepts hidden behind these tried-and-true literary terms, and so I was glad to know them. At the very least, if editors or reviewers called my central character too flat or praised the roundness of my minor characters, I was glad I knew what they were talking about.

Simply put, a minor character gets less space in print than the others. A central character gets more. This is often an arbitrary call. Think of the controversy over who gets nominated in the best actor versus the best supporting actor category at the Oscars. In the same vein, a flat character, whenever he appears, from the beginning to the end of a story or novel, is always the same. He is immune to change because he has no contradictions in his personality. He is like a stick of butter or a bar of baker's chocolate, the same thing all the way through. A round character, on the other hand, is someone who either does change in the course of a story or whose makeup contains certain tensions or inherent contradictions that make him resemble more closely a real human being. Think of the first as a stock part, the latter as a part that calls for a skilled actor. But few characters are entirely flat, while none are as round as people we know well in real life. If a fictional person were really as complicated as a real one, a novel about her life would run a million pages.

Personally I find it is more useful not to think in the extremes suggested by these terms, but rather to imagine characters as existing on a continuum. They are positioned along a sliding scale that runs from minor and flat (say a brief wordless appearance) to central and round (appearing in every scene of a short story or novel named after them). Suppose you have a bellboy who delivers a room service breakfast and never reappears in the story. He is about as flat and minor as you can get but is worth perhaps a touch of characterization: "The bellboy frowned at the quarter Hammish had given him, then turned briskly on one heel and left."

Mrs. Pardiggle in *Bleak House* fits the definition both of a minor and a flat character almost to perfection. Dickens makes clear she is what she is, an unwanted visitor and knocker-over of small chairs, and she is not likely to take on more importance by revealing unexpected inner tensions and conflicts or suddenly bursting forth in displays of growth or change. That doesn't mean that while she is on the scene she shouldn't be both colorful and memorable.

Earlier in the same novel, Dickens introduces Mrs. Jellyby. She does not play one of the central roles, but neither is she as minor as Mrs. Pardiggle. From the beginning she is portrayed less simply, and indeed she is the embodiment of a contradiction. She is devoted to saving the bodies and souls of the natives of Boorio-boola-Gha, while at the same time she turns a blind eye to the chaos and filth of her own household and the welfare of her husband and children, which eventually results in tragic consequences. Mrs. Jellyby does not experience change or enlightenment in the course of *Bleak House*, but her contradictions make her a more rounded character than Mrs. Pardiggle and a more interesting one.

So even with fairly flat or minor characters, making one trait stand in opposition to another (appearance contradicting speech, speech belying actions) makes for more interesting reading. If our lawyer at the party in the beginning of this chapter wore an Armani suit and still handed out cards that read *1-800-Sue-Them*, he might be more interesting for the contradiction. Or he might hand out his card, then spend the whole evening talking about feeding the homeless or writing sonnets.

The more central a character, the more likely he is to be the narrator or the point-of-view character, and then interior development becomes key. If he has conflicts and contradictions that appear on the surface, those are usually amplified and explained in his thoughts. Many of the most memorable central characters seem all of a piece on the outside—quiet, ordinary, even dully conformist—and only come alive when viewed from the inside. Holden Caulfield *is* his interior life.

If a central character is neither a narrator nor a point-of-view character, his interior life cannot be shown directly. Therefore great care must be taken to build up a complete portrait of him from the outside. As I pointed out earlier, Jay Gatsby does not tell his own story in *The Great Gatsby*; Nick Carraway tells it. Because he chooses a peripheral narrator, Fitzgerald must use Nick's accounts of Gatsby's actions and speech as well as the stories told about Gatsby by others to give a complete picture of the mysterious, doomed bootlegger. Despite this distance, I doubt there has been a more compelling central character or a more rounded one written in this century.

REVEALING YOURSELF ON THE PAGE

Up to this point we've concentrated on technique, on how character as a structural element can be built on the page. But there is a less easily managed side to fiction, something that can hinder or help your creation of a world full of people invented just by you, or at least rendered by you from life with the names changed to protect the innocent. Remember that everything you have learned from observing your parents, friends, enemies, and lovers is filtered through the prism of who you are and that this shapes the people you create. This means that what you write inevitably reveals who you *really* are, even if you don't want it to. That's the scary part. If your view of the world is mean or petty or just plain boring, no trick of description or dialogue will hide that. Much more than what you wear, you are what you write.

A friend of mine, a graduate student in English, read my novel, *The Museum of Happiness*, and then handed me a list of equations he'd made while he was reading. *Cleanliness = death*, he wrote. *Doctors = evil. Mothers are cold or vengeful. Fathers kind but weak or distant. Sex = salvation.* "It would make an interesting paper, don't you think?" he asked. I looked over the list and nodded faintly. What he'd written seemed true enough in connection with my novel when I thought about it, though like most writers I hadn't been operating on such an analytical level when I was writing. The frightening thing was that his notes could easily have been made by a psychologist about my own life: *cold mother, distant father. The Museum of Happiness* is set in Paris in 1929. I honestly thought I'd made up the characters.

Oh well, I thought, the scholars have a fine time puzzling over the effect that Hemingway's sexuality, Flannery O'Connor's brand of Catholicism, and Twain's attitude toward blacks and women might or might not have had on the people they created. If I'm lucky enough to write something that continues to be read, I'll leave these concerns to later generations. But my friend's list also occasioned a bout of soul-searching. My personal writing nightmare is that my fiction will reach a wall where it can't get any better because the flaws in my personality are also the flaws in my fiction. I'd be unable to see them, much less fix them.

While I worked on *The Museum of Happiness*, I hit just such a wall. There are two central point-of-view characters: Roland Keppi, a half-Alsatian, half-German carnival worker, and Ginny Gillespie, a young

Floridian who moves to Paris. I had a terrible time writing, not the Roland sections, about a man with whom I have nothing in common, but the Ginny sections. I was born in France and raised in Florida, the opposite of Ginny, but it was still too close for comfort. I, too, was a young woman (one with a mother and father who resembled hers). In many ways I was Ginny. And for reasons too deep for me to unknot, I didn't like her. It kept showing. The passages in the novel about her were duller than others because they were less fleshed out. I didn't give her much to say in dialogue, and I couldn't seem to describe her or her motivations convincingly. I finally pulled the old trick of changing a character physically to distance her from reality. I have blond hair. I turned Ginny into a redhead. Somehow that worked well enough for me to go back and add the pieces of her personality that were missing. I was able to finish the book.

It also made me turn to memoir for my next project, a book called *Space* about growing up near Cape Kennedy during the moon race. I thought it was the only way to confront, and perhaps conquer, my inability to sympathize with or write about someone who was too much like me. Also I thought it would be cheaper than years of psychoanalysis. I was willing to do this because I don't want any character to be beyond my understanding, not even my own, because I believe that convincing characters are the most important part of any novel or short story.

Literary fiction is often said to be character driven as opposed to the plot-driven world of the genres. But even in mysteries, character is central. How else can you explain the popularity of the many mystery series with book after book featuring the same detective? Arthur Conan Doyle bitterly lamented the public's demand for ever more appearances of his sleuth Sherlock Holmes and readers' failure to appreciate what Doyle felt were his more important, now largely forgotten, historical novels. For better or worse, in Holmes he had created a character so memorable that he took on a life of his own. He would later appear in books, plays, and films in situations never imagined in the wildest dreams of Sir Arthur (side by side with Sigmund Freud, suspected by Watson of being Jack the Ripper, even fighting Nazi spies). As a writer my dream is to create characters so real that like children they will outlive me to join Holmes and Holden Caulfield and David Copperfield and Kurtz on the long list of characters so vividly realized by their authors that they have become part of the lives of generations of readers.

EXERCISES

1. To create a person on the page, answer these ten questions with simple one-word or one-sentence answers. If it helps, you can use a picture from a magazine or newspaper or spot some stranger on the street and use your first impression to get you going.

A. Give your character a name. If you have ever had to name a pet or a child, you know this is an important decision. It will influence not only how your readers think of the character, but also how you do. If you get stuck, flip open the phone book. Baby-naming books with their long lists of first names are also great.

B. Give your character one telling item of clothing. You don't need to describe everything, just the one item that might suggest the whole outfit. (A black leather coat, for example, or a pink, plaid jacket.)

C. Give your character one small, revealing gesture or movement. (He may bite his nails. She may cross and recross her legs.)

D. Write down one expression or line of dialogue that your character says regularly, such as a favorite curse or bit of slang.

E. Think of a smell to go with your character, like cigarette smoke or baby powder.

F. Give your character a favorite possession small enough to be carried.

G. What is your character's earliest memory?

H. Happiest memory?

I. Most painful memory?

J. If your character were dying, what would her last thought be?

2. Review your list. Now change at least one exterior detail to make it stand in opposition to the others. (Your character is wearing a filthy raincoat but smells of expensive perfume.) Change one of the interior details to make it stand in opposition to an exterior one. (Your character is carrying a small Bible, but her most painful memory is her mother's forcing her down on her knees to ask God's forgiveness for being born in sin.)

3. Now make another ten-item list, this time flattening a real person, someone you know well, into a character. Remember this is fiction. If you don't know this person's most painful memory, make it up.

4. Make one last list, only this time use yourself as the model.

5. Compare these three characters. Which is the most convincing?

CHAPTER SIX

CONFLICT IN FICTION

I t's time to step back and draw up a plan. You thought long and hard until you had a wonderful idea, then you wrote an opening and chose a point of view. Before you go any farther, you must make sure your fiction has a structure that fits your characters and the situation in which you have placed them. You do this by planning a believable and clearly developed conflict.

My first writing teacher was the novelist Janet Burroway. I took her class a number of years before she wrote her widely used text *Writing Fiction*, but her theories of narrative were already well evolved, and I was lucky enough to hear her make her points in person with the aid of an old blackboard. When I think about how to build a story, I often hear Burroway's voice.

She subscribes to the classic theory that story structure is conflict based. She takes as her model a theory about drama developed by the German playwright Gustav Freytag called the Freytag Pyramid, often represented as an equilateral triangle. For him every play begins with a conflict, continues until there is a crisis, and ends as the conflict is resolved as the result of the crisis. Because the crisis in fiction usually comes near the end of a short story or novel, Burroway lengthened and flattened out the incline of the first side of Freytag's pyramid, drawing it with an authoritative squeak of chalk on the blackboard as an inverted check mark. It looked like the illustration on the next page.

Burroway used the fairy tale "Cinderella" to explain this theory. She urged us to call out the details of the plot, and we did, freely mixing the

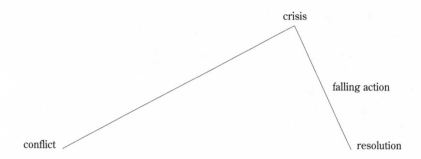

bloodier details provided by the Brothers Grimm with Disney's happy mice. We decided the conflict was that Cinderella wanted to go to the ball, but her stepmother wouldn't let her. The crisis that ended the conflict was Cinderella's foot sliding into that famous glass slipper. The falling action was that the prince and Cinderella got married. The resolution? They lived happily ever after, an ending that at nineteen we all envied.

By the time we finished, we all felt we had done a good hour's work. Even then I sensed that just as no story is as complex as real life, there is no model of narrative structure, no possible diagram of plot, that completely captures the intricacies of fiction. By its very nature any model simplifies as well as clarifies. Every model of how a story works comes complete with the kind of exceptions that plague English spelling (*i* before *e* except after *c* except in neighbor, etc.). Still the true test for any writing theory is its usefulness. Does it help you write your story? For me the conflict model of plot and structure has proven itself time and time again. I have found myself returning to this idea of strife as the engine of narrative, modifying and elaborating on it as my own knowledge of what I was trying to do in my fiction deepened.

THE CONFLICT FORMULA

There is a formula that defines the conflict in a story: It occurs when someone (A) wants something (B) and someone or something (C) frustrates that desire. Cinderella (A) wants to go to the ball (B). Her stepmother (C) is keeping her from going. This formula sent me back to the list of possible conflicts that are a fixture in most high school literature texts: man versus nature, man versus man, man versus self.

With the last of these, I ran up against the central problem of using Cinderella as a model for the conflicts I might have in my own stories or that I might find in modern fiction. Cinderella doesn't really have a self, or at least she has no inner struggles like those implied by *man versus self*. Fairy tales, like many narrative forms from oral tradition, have characters based on archetypes, characters who represent good or evil, cleverness or stupidity. They are all one thing with none of the other.

Cinderella is Good. She is unfailingly kind to animals, always a sure sign of goodness, and she is even good to her tormentors, the stepmother and stepsisters. In addition to wanting to go to the ball, she may want love (the prince) or equality (with her stepsisters and the other women invited to the ball), but Cinderella is not in a battle with herself about these desires. In other words Cinderella may want love, but it is not Cinderella that is keeping herself from getting it. At least this seems to be the case in the traditional versions of the tale. Perhaps she has conflicts that the authorial point of view traditionally used in fairy tales, a point of view that never goes into her consciousness, does not reveal. Writers are always revising and updating myths. If I wanted to rewrite Cinderella, what sort of conflicted self could I give her? Perhaps after years of abuse, she does not believe she deserves love. How would that affect the model my teacher had drawn on the board?

In that case there is a potential for two separate conflicts in the structure of any story, one external, one internal. Cinderella's external conflict is that she wants to go to the ball, but her stepmother won't let her. Her internal conflict is that she wants love but doesn't think she deserves it. The longer I thought about this more complicated model, the more I became convinced that every story has two separate conflicts that could be developed, always both an *internal* and an *external* one.

Thinking about the existence of Cinderella's internal struggle made me realize something about the external conflict as well. All the other women in the kingdom are invited to the ball, and Cinderella wants to go, too. That is what gets the story rolling, but halfway through Cinderella does get to the ball. Is the story over now that the first conflict is resolved? No. Now the complications really start. She wants to leave the ball before her dress turns back into rags, her coach into a pumpkin, and so on. In Cinderella, as in most fiction, the opening external conflict shifts. One problem leads to the next. *Joe wants to wake up and get out of bed, but he has a bad hangover. He finally does get up, in desperate need of a cup of coffee, but finds he hasn't got any. He goes to the store, but the cashier, burned by a bad check Joe wrote the week before, won't take any more. So Joe decides to go home and get his gun and rob the store, but . . .*

Even when the external conflict stays the same throughout a story, say a character is trying to win a foot race, there are stages to the conflict. *Joe wants to win and to win he knows he has to get out of the blocks fast. He does, but knows that to stay ahead he has to stay tight in the turn. He does, but . . .*

Other parts of the structure of the external conflict can shift or vary in the course of a story. The someone who wants something can stay the same while the someone or something that foils the desire changes. Through much of the story, Cinderella's external conflict could be defined as Cinderella versus the stepmother (who forbids her to go to the ball, locks her away to keep her from trying on the glass slipper), but the stepmother isn't the only one blocking Cinderella. It is not the stepmother who turns the coachmen back into mice. The fairy godmother's magic comes with a set of rules, and those rules keep Cinderella from staying at the ball with the prince and getting what she wants. This does not mean the external conflict has no continuity. If that were true, the story of Cinderella would seem like just one darn thing after another, more like life perhaps but too loose a structure for fiction. In this case the continuity is reinforced when the story returns in the end to its focus on the stepmother.

These variations in the conflict of a simple fairy tale make it a richer story, and the clear implication is that more sophisticated fiction should also have complications that change and evolve. A story combining struggles of man against man with man against nature will be more interesting than a story with a simple solitary villain. That's why *Moby Dick* has Captain Ahab *and* the white whale.

CRISIS ACTION

External conflict is always resolved by a visible *crisis action*, no matter how small that action may be. Readers must be able to see the crisis action. It must happen in the external world of the story, like the runner winning the race or Cinderella sliding her foot into the slipper. In any work of fiction, the crisis action naturally comes near the end, but in contemporary short stories it often comes so near the end that our pyramidal structure is hardly a pyramid at all. It's more of a ramp that ends abruptly.

crisis

falling action

resolution

conflict

In Michelle Herman's short story "Auslander," the central character is tempted to translate the work of a poet who has asked that her work be destroyed. In the end Auslander finds she cannot disobey the poet's wishes, leading to these last two sentences of the story.

> With one arm she held the poet's work; with her free hand she pulled open the door to the incinerator chute. It was a matter of seconds; then it was done.

The crisis action is opening the door to the incinerator chute. The falling action, "It was a matter of seconds." The resolution (happily or unhappily ever after), "then it was done." All in two sentences. Sometimes in a short story the crisis action is in the last sentence. The only falling action and resolution occur in the readers' minds. In this abbreviated structure, the crisis action tells us how the conflict will end, whether the character will get what she wants, and readers are left to imagine whether she lived happily or unhappily ever after.

As a general rule, the longer the work of fiction, the more falling action and resolution are needed. The more time we spend with characters, the more we want to know just where we are leaving them. A character in a short story can be left on the edge of change. But novels make us want to see the change happen, to see the person's life settled for better or worse. In novels the crisis action is often in the next-to-last chapter. The classic mystery novel with its plot-driven narrative provides a clear example of this. In the next-to-last chapter, the murderer may be revealed, shot, or arrested (crisis action). Then comes the last chapter in which the detective explains how he knew who did it and points out all of the clues (falling action), and any subplots of romance or reconciliation between the characters are concluded (resolution).

RESOLVING INTERNAL CONFLICT

If exterior conflicts are resolved by an exterior crisis action, it is equally true that interior conflicts are resolved inside a character or in some secondary reflection of a character's interior thoughts, such as dialogue or analysis by a narrator or author. If Cinderella's inner conflict is *Am I worthy of love?* then the internal crisis occurs when she decides to put her foot in the shoe and risk being recognized and loved by the prince. The crisis is the moment she decides to act. This may be preceded and reinforced by memory. She could remember a kind act by her dead father, the prince, or her fairy godmother, or a cruelty inflicted by her stepsisters or stepmother. Her internal crisis could be accompanied by an image that brings enlightenment or a vision. She could see light streaming through the window, think she hears her father's beloved voice or the mice singing "Here Comes the Bride." Any or all of this is fair game in setting up her decision, making it believable and clear to your readers. These subtler manifestations of her internal state may lead her to think explicitly, "I deserve love," or they may stand in place of any such direct thought on her part. Either way the internal crisis takes place inside a character, and that leads to the external crisis action.

Honestly, without the struggle going on inside them, who cares whether the ragged girl's foot fits the shoe or the runner wins or loses the race? We care only if we know what is at stake for the girl or the runner. This is certainly the case in English author Alan Sillitoe's "The Loneliness of the Long-Distance Runner." The narrator opens by telling us:

> As soon as I got to Borstal they made me a long-distance cross-country runner. I suppose they thought I was just the build for it . . . and in any case I didn't mind it much, to tell you the truth, because running had always been made much of in our family, especially running away from the police.

The narrator knows the authorities at his reform school want him to run for them, not for himself, but he also loves to run. So when the day of the big race comes, we know both the external conflict (will he win the race?) and the internal one (if he wins he is selling out to the school's governor). The resolution to the interior battle comes when the narrator decides to lose the race and feels nothing but joy.

I could hear the lords and ladies now from the grandstand. . . . "Run!" they were shouting in their posh voices.
"Run!" But I . . . stood where I was . . . blubbing now out of
gladness that I'd got them beat at last.

The resolution to the exterior conflict, the crisis action, is when a
competitor passes him, breaks the tape, and wins the race. The wonderful thing about the end of the race in "The Loneliness of the Long-
Distance Runner" is that, like the glass slipper in "Cinderella," it works
neatly within the story structure to resolve both the interior and exterior conflicts.

BALANCING EXTERNAL AND INTERNAL CONFLICT

In "Auslander," "The Loneliness of the Long-Distance Runner," and
our reworked version of "Cinderella," the external and internal conflicts are parallel structures to keep readers reading and to make the
fiction memorable. Inevitably in some works the exterior conflict is
more important, in others the interior. Stories exist along a continuum.
At one end some emphasize the external almost exclusively (a character swimming for the world record), and at the other end are ones
that emphasize the internal (a character trying to decide whether to
commit suicide). Most fall somewhere in between.

When you consider the possible conflicts of your characters, you
should know what each type can and cannot do for you. External
conflict gets readers into a story. In chapter two, the opening I called
Into the Pot, Already Boiling is based on immediate external conflict:
A man is driving somewhere and driving fast. In this sense it is probably
what most people mean when they say plot. *This happened, then that
happened, then this.* It is what you hear when someone tries to summa-
rize the plot of a movie. *This guy has to get to Denver by midnight. He's
making good time, but then he has a flat tire. This woman stops to help
him, but . . .* Always there is a *but,* usually a string of them. This
struggle and its ensuing complications seesaw up and down. One
minute someone is going to get what he wants, the next he isn't.

John Cheever's short story "The Country Husband" opens with
an immediate external conflict: "To begin at the beginning, the airplane from Minneapolis in which Francis Weed was traveling East

ran into heavy weather." The situation grows rapidly worse until the plane begins to go down.

> The stewardess announced that they were going to make an emergency landing. All but the child saw in their minds the spreading wings of the Angel of Death. The pilot could be heard singing faintly, "I've got sixpence, jolly, jolly sixpence. I've got sixpence to last me all my life...."

Francis Weed and the other passengers and crew do not die. The plane lands, they get off, and there is not even an explosion. Taxis come to carry them to the train and life goes on. Francis is left struggling to explain his near-death experience to a friend.

This reversal of fortune rhythm to external conflict—two steps forward, one step back—is so ingrained, I often give my students a round-robin exercise. I number a sheet of paper from one to fifteen (the number of students in my workshops) then start it around the table. The first person has to give a character a desire, the second frustrate it, the third help to make it seem possible again, the fourth complicate the situation once more. The paper usually gets all the way around, but not always. One memorable round stopped with student number four.

1. A man wants to be a concert pianist.
2. Then he loses an arm.
3. Luckily he meets another piano player with one arm.
4. Unfortunately it is the same arm.

Here we have the perfect example of the limitations of external conflict. Because this conflict and its ensuing complications are all external, the second complication stopped the story dead in its tracks. The only possibilities seemed too absurd for an upturn in fortune: *Luckily he learned to play concerts with his toes.*

However, if this story has a parallel internal conflict, you can go on with it. He wants to play the piano professionally, but his loss of an arm stops him. On the inside his thoughts may be quite different. He may know he needs to learn to live without the piano but feels he is worthless without it. He wants to change but can't. The other one-armed piano player, the one who can't solve the external conflict (no duets with two right hands), can help solve the internal problem. He can show our struggling disabled pianist how to play with one hand or, by setting a good example, how to live a full life as an ex-piano player or, by bad example, what lies ahead of him if he wallows in drugged or drunken self-pity. The true outcome of the story depends on what is happening in our first one-armed piano player's head, what thoughts, memories, fantasies, and resolutions are sparked by the situation and how these bring about the solution to the battle within himself.

This does not mean that the resolution to the external conflict is unimportant. Finding just the right glass slipper is key to making a story memorable and the resolution of the internal conflict believable. The incinerator makes a very final end for the poet's work in "Auslander." The central character cannot weaken and retrieve the papers. Sometimes the most effective crisis action is small and symbolic. If a character throws open a window, she may be opening herself to change; if she shuts one, closing herself off. Our piano player might close the piano or open it, let his wife touch him or turn away.

THE NEED FOR ACTION

About the same time I started to ponder the state of Cinderella's soul, I taught a literature course that started with the King James Version of the Old Testament, full of characters whose interiors are as closed to us as Cinderella's, and ran through Virginia Woolf, whose characters seem nearly all interior. We had just started on *Hamlet* whose main character is more conflicted than most in Western literature. Hamlet's exterior conflict is clear. The ghost of his dead father asks Hamlet to avenge his father's murder by Uncle Claudius who is now king, and the killing of a king brings with it certain inevitable external problems. But scholars do not write volumes about the difficulties of Hamlet's actually bringing a sword to bear on Claudius, though the complications are real enough. Hamlet stabs a man behind his mother's curtain sure it is his uncle Claudius, only to find he has killed Polonius, the king's counselor and the father of the woman he loves. But as my students never fail to point out to me, *Hamlet* is a long play, and the prince has many opportunities to get revenge for his father's murder. It is not mere superficial complications that keep him from getting the job done. It is Hamlet's inner struggle that causes scholars to write and argue endlessly. Why can't Hamlet act? Why does it take him the entire play to avenge his father's murder?

Clearly Hamlet is a character at war with himself. He is the someone who keeps himself from doing what he wants, and his indecision is complex. This complexity makes Hamlet a good model for internal conflict. Nineteenth-century poet and critic Samuel Taylor Coleridge believed Hamlet suffers from "an overbalance in the contemplative faculty." He can't act because he thinks too much. He was, after all, a university student. He is more like a character in contemporary fiction than one like Cinderella who thinks too little. More recent critics believe Hamlet has an existential dilemma to resolve. He cannot take vengeance for his father's murder until he can convince himself that it would be truly right to do so, that his uncle's death would make a difference, that justice is possible in such an imperfect world. He cannot act until he is convinced there is a point in acting. Contemporary fiction is full of characters whose main obstacle to happiness, to love, to a new and better life, is their failure to believe change is possible. In this case the resolution to Hamlet's internal conflict, like Cinderella's, is that he must decide to act. That does not happen until the final scene, in which the stage is literally piled with bodies, one of them Hamlet's.

For writers the interesting point about Hamlet's internal conflicts is not which critic has got it right, but that his struggle has held readers' and playgoers' attention for four hundred years because it is both complicated and has consequence (all those dead bodies). Beware of a person whose desires fit too simply into the conflict formula; we want rounded characters, not cartoons. Also remember that Hamlet does finally act. If a character errs too far on the side of thinking over action, you may have on your hands what Jerome Stern in *Making Shapely Fiction* calls a bathtub story. That is one so devoid of external conflict, indeed of any action, that it is like watching someone mulling over her life while taking a nice, long, hot, boring bath.

MANY VIEWPOINTS, MANY CONFLICTS

I've mentioned that having two central point-of-view characters is common for novels, though some short stories have more than one as well. If Cinderella's story were told from both Cinderella's and the prince's points of view, they would each have their own external and internal conflicts (yes, that makes four pyramids). If the story were told from Cinderella's, the prince's, and the wicked stepmother's points of view, there would be three sets of conflicts. You can see how every viewpoint you add complicates a story. Using *Cinderella*, let's see how these conflicts might work in a story with multiple points of view.

The three opening external conflicts:

- Cinderella wants to go to the ball.
- The stepmother doesn't want Cinderella to go.
- The prince doesn't want to go because it's his father's way of finding him a wife.

The internal conflicts might run like this:

- Cinderella wants love but doesn't think she deserves it.
- The stepmother wants her daughters to triumph over Cinderella but knows this is wicked.
- The prince wants love but feels duty will make this impossible.

Just when handling so many points of view might seem to make the story hopelessly complex, we are saved, as was Cinderella, by the glass slipper. The glass slipper is the crisis action for Cinderella, the prince, *and* the stepmother. The trick with resolving everyone's internal conflict in a story with multiple points of view (since we can only be in one person's head at the end) is to have established ahead of time the consequences of the crisis action. Thus even without revisiting each character's mind, we know that the resolution for Cinderella and the prince is that they live happily ever after and that the stepmother lives unhappily ever after.

USING THE CONFLICT MODEL

Don't be disheartened if all this advice seems a bit much to think about. I am not suggesting you diagram each story before you write it. This would be a bad idea, one likely to stifle creativity and result in predictable stories. One way to use technical information about writing is to internalize it, to make it part of you by knowing the information well enough to draw on it without having to stop and think, in the way a jazz musician knows chords, a gymnast her moves. It is almost instinctive for me to use the conflict-crisis-resolution structure for plotting. As I am walking the dog, doing dishes, or taking a shower, I use it while thinking over the ideas I have for a story. I ask myself, Where will the story start? (What is the opening exterior conflict?) What does my character want? (What interior conflict?)

Where is the story headed? (What crisis action?) Often by the time I actually start writing a story, I have a single concluding image in my mind that I write toward. It is the story's glass slipper.

I never know every complication, every reversal of my character's progress. I discover those as I go along, rather like my class did in the exercise that brought us the one-handed piano player. If I knew every difficulty in advance, I would be too bored to bother writing the story. If I did go ahead and write it, my boredom would be communicated to readers who would in turn be bored. As I walk around half in the world and half in my own head deciding on a basic plot for a story, the process of shaping it feels organic, visceral. If I were asked to describe the process, I would use metaphors like working in clay or even plumping a pillow. I would never say it feels like filling in a form or writing an outline. If I started to think about a story in process in those terms, I would take it as a sign of trouble.

The second way to use technical information such as the conflict model of plot is in revision. Here it can be invoked more consciously. If I am lucky, if all my plumping and shaping has worked, a story comes out of its first draft with a good, clear working plot and overall structure. More often, only some things work. The details of the marathon run in a story are tense and well told, but no one I ask to read my draft has any idea who the narrator really is or what she might want beyond simply coming in first. Or everyone is drawn to my young, vulnerable, needy central character, but the final scene is so confusing no one knows whether her turning on her radio means she is going to swallow that overdose of sleeping pills or not. At this point I often do make diagrams, plotting out on paper or in my head each complication in both the external and internal conflicts. I do this to give myself a clear idea of what to change or keep in the next draft. Then I start writing again, trying to make my story work from first word to last.

EXERCISES

1. Choose a story that you know well, a family story or fairy tale, and write the answers to these questions.

    A. First, whose story is it? (Who is the someone who wants something?)

    B. What does the character want? Immediately (opening external conflict) and on a deeper, emotional level (internal conflict). If you are drawing on a family story or a fairy tale, you will probably have to invent or intuit the internal conflict just as we did with Cinderella.

C. On the external level of the plot, who or what is keeping her from getting what she wants? On the internal?

D. What are the complications both external and internal that move the plot forward? (Now she is going to get it. Now she isn't.)

E. What is the moment in the story when we know for certain she is or is not going to get what she wants. What is the character thinking, feeling, and imagining at that moment? What is the external crisis action (the glass slipper)?

2. Look over your answers. Is this a story worth writing?

3. Do the exercise again, this time using as a source either a short story you have already written or an idea for a story you want to write.

CHAPTER SEVEN

CONTINUING CONFLICT

We have been following the path into fiction, taking up the elements of structure in the order they would arise in the writing of a single short story or novel. Let's assume that you already have chosen the materials you'll need for your story, the characters, point of view, and the external and internal conflicts that will hook your readers in the first few paragraphs or pages. You have made a good beginning and know what the end will look like. Next you must write the rest of the story, developing your conflicts, filling in the distance from the initial conflict to the final resolution.

The trick to keeping your story moving is to simultaneously advance both the exterior and interior conflicts, making them work together. Although your work is headed toward a final showdown, there will be many smaller ups and downs along the way in which external problems will begin to seem solvable and then become more implacable than ever, while internally the character alternates between hope and disappointment. Let's look at some strategies for handling both the conflicts. Then at the end of this chapter, I'll mention a few extras you might consider using to keep your reader's interest.

External conflict is always based on action, and action in fiction is organized in two basic ways: You can make your characters move through space or through time. Many short stories and most novels use a combination of the two, but often one predominates. Either someone is going somewhere, and progress is measured by milestones passed, or someone is given a limited time to do something, and progress is measured by how much gets done. A race is an example of space traveled and time used being equally important, a leisurely walk around the block an example of space covered, and a three-hour SAT examination a pure example of time spent. We'll look at some examples so you can see how each method works to advance external conflict. Likewise there are two basic ways to deepen internal conflict. A character can respond to an event with thoughts about the current situation or with thoughts about some other time (flashbacks or dreams or visions).

EXTERNAL CONFLICT DEVELOPMENT
Movement Through Space

Journeys are one of art's great gifts to a writer because they naturally provide a series of external conflicts. Characters have some place they need to be, and any trip involves potential complications (they can get lost, robbed, or snowed in). Even an everyday trip can be full of hazards. Erin McGraw's "A Suburban Story" begins with an ill-fated drive to school.

> When the pebble flew out from the gravel truck in front of them and cracked the windshield, Iris wasn't even looking; she had leaned over to tighten her daughter's seat belt. She jerked her head up at the sharp pop and looked into a lattice of hard lines. Lisa, of course, started to cry.

McGraw's short story only opens with a trip, but by the time Iris delivers her daughter into the hands of her kindergarten teacher, we have learned that the mother's life in general is going every bit as badly as her morning drive.

A journey provides a perfect structure for external conflict development because it lets readers know enough of what is coming (a forty-mile drive to Grandmother's house, a hitchhike from Paris to Athens) to set comfortable expectations at the same time it doles out surprises scene by scene. In Joy Williams' short story "Train," ten-year-old Danica is traveling to Florida with her dubious best friend, Jane Muirhead, Jane's battling parents, and an assortment of odd, slightly drunk extras. We know from the outset that they are going from Washington, DC, to Florida on the train, but what will happen to her on the trip is unknown. In one scene in the train's Starlight Lounge,

Danica is surprised to hear her friend ask her parents, who fight constantly, why they aren't sitting together.

> "I am not sitting with your mother because I am sitting with this young man here. We are having a fascinating conversation."
>
> "Why are you always talking to young men?" Jane asked.
>
> "Jane, honey," Mr. Muirhead said, "I will answer that." He took a swallow of his drink and sighed. He leaned forward and said earnestly, "I talk to so many young men because your mother won't let me talk to young women."

Any difficulty Danica encounters, pettiness on Jane's part, the cynical drunken fighting of the elder Muirheads, simply makes us more worried for Danica and heightens the external tension.

All of this happens in the context of the train ride which gives readers a general sense of the duration of the story but frees them and the characters from worrying about exactly what time it is or even where they are at a particular moment. In this case travel provides a context for character development and conflict free from day-to-day worries. The characters have the space to show who they are and what they really think.

A journey in fiction does not have to involve miles. Nicholson Baker's experimental novel *The Mezzanine* opens with the narrator returning by foot to his desk after lunch.

> At almost one o'clock I entered the lobby of the building where I worked and turned toward the escalators, carrying a black Penguin paperback and a small white CVS bag, its receipt stapled over the top. The escalators rose toward the mezzanine, where my office was. . . . When I drew close to the up escalator, I involuntarily transferred my paperback and CVS bag to my left hand, so that I could take the handrail with my right, according to habit.

Baker's 135-page novel takes place as a flashback while he is traveling thirty-five or forty feet up the escalator. Between chapter one as he prepares to grasp the handrail and chapter fifteen when he looks down from the top and waves at a maintenance man, the narrator will recall his lunch hour, including walking from his desk to the men's room and later into a CVS Drugstore. In the world of Baker's minutely observed fiction, this is big action. The exterior struggles are over the smallest decisions (should the narrator buy some shoe polish? use the hand dryer in the men's room?). Such is the persuasive power of his writing that by the end of *The Mezzanine*, most readers would agree that such decisions are worth several pages of consideration. If you want to create external tension through careful attention to everyday decisions, take a lesson from Baker and describe even the smallest risks in a way that tells readers they matter.

Jack Kerouac's *On the Road* is a classic American novel whose external conflicts are organized by travel through space. It begins in New Jersey with the planning of a coast-to-coast hitchhiking trip.

> I'd been poring over maps of the United States in Paterson for months, even reading books about the pioneers and savoring names like Platte and Cimarron and so on, and on the road-map was one long red line called Route 6 that led from the tip of Cape Cod clear to Ely, Nevada, and there dipped down to Los Angeles. I'll just stay on 6 all the way to Ely, I said to myself and confidently started.

The entire novel is spent crossing and recrossing the country by foot, car, bus, and plane. Days or weeks or months are spent in Chicago, Denver, San Francisco, New Orleans, Manhattan, and Mexico City, but the restless wandering and what happens along the way is the point of the book. Kerouac creates a portrait of the country and a group of young men at the end of the 1940s. The novel comes to rest in New York.

> So in America when the sun goes down . . . I sit on the old broken-down river pier watching the long, long skies over New Jersey and sense all that raw land that rolls in one unbelievable huge bulge over to the West Coast, and all that road going, all the people dreaming in the immensity of it. . . . the evening star must be drooping and shedding her sparkler dims on the prairie, which is just before the coming of complete night that blesses the earth, darkens all rivers, cups the peaks and folds the final shore in, and nobody, nobody knows what's going to happen to anybody besides the forlorn rags of growing old. . . .

If you want to tell the truth about a lone visionary, a group of friends, a pivotal time in history, or all three, a journey like this can provide the external conflicts necessary to make your vision into a narrative instead of merely another essay on the Beat or any other generation.

Movement Through Time

We are born at one end of a time line and move down it until the day we die. If we are ever in danger of forgetting this, we have rituals like birthdays, graduations, and wedding anniversaries to remind us of where we are in the great gray march. Time passes in all fiction, too. Sometimes, as in *The Mezzanine*, it is a complement to physical motion. Time passes during Danica's trip in "Train," but it is a secondary consideration, something that serves largely to set the scope and range of the journey, to define how much space will be covered. In *On the Road* measuring time is unimportant. There are no firm deadlines for a particular hour, day, or year, just the bigger threat of time with a capital *T*—mortality.

In some types of fiction, however, time is the main organizing principle; time sets readers' expectations and controls the development of external conflict. This is particularly true in stories and novels that follow a character through a typical day. One classic example of this approach is Aleksandr Solzhenitsyn's *One Day in the Life of Ivan Denisovich*, a tale of one man among multitudes sentenced to a term in the Soviet Gulag. It opens with a clear signal that this is a novel bound by time.

> Reveille was sounded, as always, at 5 A.M.—a hammer pounding on a rail outside camp HQ. The ringing noise came faintly on and off through the windowpanes covered with ice more than an inch thick, and died away fast. It was cold and the warder didn't feel like going on banging.

The *as always* is an early clue, if we need one beyond the title, that this is a story that deals with one day's events in the camp. This is a form that allows for comment on slight variations, "It was cold and the warder didn't feel like going on banging," but will treat the most terrible details (the ice on the windowpanes) as if they were as ordinary to us as they are to Ivan Denisovich Shukhov. The external conflict here is simple: Will Ivan survive this day as he has survived the ones before it? We know we will spend a day with him, but we do not know what that day will bring, and every threat to Ivan advances the external conflict.

The book ends 209 pages later, as Ivan goes to sleep.

> Shukhov went to sleep, and he was very happy. He'd had a lot of luck today. They hadn't put him in the cooler. The gang hadn't been chased out to work in the Socialist Community Development. He'd finagled an extra bowl of mush at lunch. . . .
>
> There were three thousand six hundred and fifty three days like this in his sentence, from reveille to lights out.
>
> The three extra ones were because of the leap years. . . .

With this closing list, indicating there are 3,653 days in Ivan's sentence, Solzhenitsyn places in context the terrible meaning of this one day in Ivan Denisovich Shukhov's life. It leaves him at risk and gives us reason to think of him long after we have finished the book.

The day-in-the-life form exists for short stories as well. Stanley Elkin's short story "I Look Out for Ed Wolfe" follows the title character through a not-so-typical day. He gets fired from his job at a loan collection agency, creating an immediate external conflict.

> "All right," La Meck began, "I'm not going to lie to you."
> Lie to me. Lie to me, Ed Wolfe prayed silently.
> "You're in here for me to fire you. . . . though I like you personally I got no use for you in my office."

Ed, an orphan, finds himself suddenly cut adrift in life. How will he survive? Over the course of the day, he sells his car, closes his bank account. The external conflict turns more and more serious. Ed ends up the lone white man in a black bar with all the money he has in the world in his pocket. He has nowhere left to go. He pushes the crowd until it turns hostile, goading them toward violence by pretending to hold a slave auction of a girl in the bar. Then he throws all his money into the air. Whatever tomorrow brings for Ed Wolfe, we know it will not be a day like this one.

On a larger scale, novels and short stories can follow characters through not just one day, but a substantial portion of their lives. Again time is what defines readers' expectations for the work. The external conflict is the characters' survival, the risks—physical, moral, mental—that they face. A novel that follows a character through early or late childhood into adulthood is called a *Bildungsroman*. In these the external conflict is always the danger to the essential person, our fear that events may change the characters in ways we will regret. *Goodbye, Columbus*, Philip Roth's Jewish-American coming-of-age novel, is a particularly funny and poignant take on the form. Charles Dickens goes so far as to turn *David Copperfield*, perhaps his best-known novel, into a fake autobiography that begins with a chapter titled "I Am Born."

> Whether I shall turn out to be the hero of my own life, or whether that station will be held by anybody else, these pages must show. To begin my life with the beginning of my life, I record that I was born (as I have been informed and believe) on a Friday, at twelve o'clock at night. It was remarked that the clock began to strike, and I began to cry, simultaneously.

Dickens goes on to have chapters such as "I fall into Disgrace," "I am a New Boy in more Senses than One," and "A Light shines on my Way." Even though these novels cover a much greater span of time, we worry about David Copperfield just as we do Ivan Denisovich and Ed Wolfe. We want to see what life does to these endangered characters, and every minute, hour, day, or year brings new dangers and thus heightens external conflict.

John Updike in his Rabbit books (*Rabbit, Run; Rabbit Redux; Rabbit Is Rich; Rabbit at Rest*) follows the life of a single character from boy to man through successive novels. Philip Roth and Richard Ford have also written novels that return, after many years, to the same central character to chronicle his life. These longer chronicles work on the same principle that time brings with it risks and so advances the external conflict.

The real trick to successfully using time to both establish and advance the exterior conflict is to make clear from the beginning the nature of the time to be covered. Remember *David Copperfield* ("To begin my life with the beginning of my life"). This is true even if your use of time is an unconventional one as it is in Kurt Vonnegut's marvelously inventive novel *Slaughterhouse-Five*. Vonnegut's central character, the aptly named Billy Pilgrim, comes unstuck in time, moving randomly among the events of his life, including his time as a POW in German hands during World War II, during which he witnesses the terrible fire-bombing of Dresden. Billy does not experience time as a straight line, yet we read on, just as we do in more conventional time-based fiction, to find out what will happen to Billy, even if his existence at one point in time (as a middle-aged man) implies he survived an earlier external threat (the fire-bombing). Vonnegut establishes his complicated conception of Billy's time line by the simplest and most direct of methods. He announces it.

> Listen:
> Billy Pilgrim has come unstuck in time.
> Billy has gone to sleep a senile widower and awakened on his wedding day. He has walked through a door in 1955 and come out another one in 1941. He has gone back through that door to find himself in 1963. He has seen his birth and death many times, he says, and pays random visits to all the events in between.
> He says.

After that opening, readers are forewarned. If you want to try something similar, you should be equally direct, clear, and bold.

INTERNAL CONFLICT DEVELOPMENT
Thoughts

Remember that no matter how your external conflict is organized, the development of the internal conflict must keep pace with it. Let's say you are writing a story whose external conflict is that the central character, living in Los Angeles, must reach his mother's funeral in Idaho. This is an external conflict defined by movement through space, though you could also use time to heighten the tension, giving him a mere twenty-four hours to drive from southern California to Boise. The tension is heightened by every difficulty he runs into along the way (if his old car breaks down, if he stops for one beer and goes on to get drunk). But to first introduce and then develop the internal conflict, we need to know what these external complications mean to him. We need to get an inside view, to see his reaction to each obstacle that life or his own weakness puts in his way. We need to know what he wants and what is keeping him from getting it.

The first way we can know this is the simplest and the most common: You can give us his thoughts about what just happened. In the story about the son trying to get to his mother's funeral, it could work this way.

> The mechanic closed the hood of the Chevy, and wiped his hands on a rag. "I sure wouldn't be driving a car with an oil leak this bad no where as far as Idaho."
> Sonny shrugged. *He didn't really have a choice. He had to get to his mother's funeral. For once in his life he was going to be a good son.* "Hey, call me a gambler."

I've italicized Sonny's thoughts so you can see the pattern. The external conflict is advanced by the mechanic. The car is a piece of junk and probably won't make it to Idaho. What the son thinks in response, *For once in his life he was going to be a good son,* advances the internal conflict.

Elkin does the same thing in the scene from "I Look Out for Ed Wolfe," which we examined earlier.

> "All right," La Meck began, "I'm not going to lie to you."
> *Lie to me. Lie to me, Ed Wolfe prayed silently.*

Ed's reaction is immediate. He does not want to hear what La Meck is about to tell him. Ed's thoughts are presented in fairly simple language, but a character's thoughts can also be more impressionistic. At the end of "I Look Out for Ed Wolfe," the girl Ed has been pretending to sell as a slave reaches out and takes his hand. He looks down at her brown hand and sees

> the fine articulation of bones, the rich sudden rush of muscle. Inside her own he saw, indifferently, his own pale hand, lifeless and serene, still and infinitely free.

That this more impressionistic response takes place at the end of the short story is no accident. As the internal conflict develops and becomes more complex, the language responds. The later in a story a thought appears, in language plain or fancy, the more important it is to the eventual resolution of the internal conflict, to the moment when the character either realizes or fails to realize the true nature of his situation.

Dreams

The second device for developing internal conflict is the use of thoughts less directly tied to the immediate external conflict. An event can set off a flashback, a memory. Less often it can provoke a vision of the future or a dream that brings to the surface the subconscious mind. These techniques can provide important information about the true nature of the internal conflict.

In a flashback a character remembers something from the past. It can consist of a quickly remembered image or scrap of dialogue of a few sentences or a paragraph. Or it can be a more complete scene with extended dialogue and action that lasts for many pages, even for entire chapters or sections of a novel. The first time flashback is used in the work, it may be announced by a *he remembered* or similar clue. Say our son on his way to the funeral is reflecting on his mother.

> He *remembered* one early Sunday morning before church. His mother had been the one to wake him. Together, they snuck down to the kitchen to start the coffee. It was his job to measure out the twelve scoops, fragrant, brown as loose dirt, into the big percolator.

If the device is used often in a story, the use of clues like the word *remembered* quickly becomes unnecessary. After a stop to fill up with gas and get a cup of coffee, the son could have a flashback like this.

> He put his travel mug in the cup holder and pulled back onto the highway. What a mess he and his mother had made fixing breakfast that Sunday. Flour was everywhere. He tried to break the eggs into the batter one-handed, but he dropped four in a row on the floor. His mother had only laughed and dropped a fifth on the floor for good measure.
>
> He took a long swallow of coffee. He was making good time, in spite of stopping, and would easily get to the funeral by noon.

Notice that the transition from the present time of the story to the past is signalled by a simple change in verb tense. In this case the story is told in past tense, so to step farther back in time, we need to go from there (he *put* his travel mug in the cup holder) to past perfect (he and his mother *had made*). That establishes that you are in an earlier past, and from that point you can use the regular past tense (flour *was* everywhere). The transition back to the story's present time can be accomplished the same way, one sentence with past perfect (his mother *had* only *laughed*), then use the simple past (he *took* a long swallow). The reference to the coffee is an extra confirmation that the story has returned to its normal time.

If a story is told in present tense, you can use past tense for the whole flashback or use it only in the transition as we did with the past perfect.

> He passes another logging truck, holding his breath until he is back in the right lane. He is a careful driver. His mother drove like a mad woman. She never signalled. Once she passed an entire funeral procession in a no passing zone. She was singing as she speeded by, waving at the bereaved family. Though in honor of the occasion she chose a song that went, "What a friend we have in Jesus," instead of her favorite, "I didn't know the gun was loaded, and I'll never ever do it again." Just thinking about it, he starts to laugh.

It is also possible to use white space, instead of verb tenses, to signal the end of a flashback. The larger the amount of time spent in the past the more likely the sections are separated from each other by white space or by chapter breaks than by the more direct transitions discussed above.

This is also true of visions and dreams as devices for developing internal conflict. After pulling into a rest stop, our son could fall asleep and have a dream.

> He was so tired. Just a few minutes and he'd get back on the road. He stretched out on the front seat of the Chevy, closed his eyes. Suddenly he was already in Idaho, standing in the windy cemetery where his father was buried, where the big double tombstone stood waiting to mark the last resting place of his mother as well. But she wasn't lying in any coffin. She was sitting on a folding chair, one set up for the funeral, filing her nails. She looked up at him, shook her head. "No way," she said, waving one hand at the brown, grassless expanse of the cemetery. A cold wind stirred the dust. "I'm going

to Florida." He opened his mouth to argue, but before he could say a word, he was back in the car.

His falling asleep complicates the external conflict by raising the possibility he will be late for the funeral. Then the dream gives us information that deepens the internal conflict.

The main distinction between a dream and a vision is that a character is usually clearly asleep when dreaming. Visions tend to come to the wide eyed. Imagine a scene similar to the one above, but with Sonny awake, not asleep. Suppose he is at the funeral.

> He sat listening as the minister went on and on about what a good Christian woman his mother had been, how she'd always put the needs of others before her own. Then the sun, which had been behind a cloud, broke out and sent a single beam of light down into the dusty brown cemetery. Suddenly his mother was there, in one of the empty folding chairs, filing her nails. Sonny looked around. No one else seemed to see her. The minister droned on. His mother looked up from her manicure. "Don't believe a word he says," she said to Sonny. "I never did a damn thing I didn't want to do, and the thing I loved about you is that you didn't either." She winked at him. "So what are you doing hanging around here?" He opened his mouth to explain, but before he could say a word, she was gone.

Again the pattern begins with an external action, the minister's speaking, which sets off the vision advancing the internal conflict.

In some cases visions function as flash-forwards, peeks into the future, either as it will be or as the character fears or hopes it might become. Visions therefore often appear near the ends of stories. This is the case in Flannery O'Connor's short story "Revelation." Mrs. Turpin, a religious but self-righteous white farmer's wife, has a final vision showing that all her pride in her place in society is misplaced. She sees the sun going down over the trees and then a swinging bridge extending upward.

> Upon it a vast horde of souls were rumbling toward heaven. There were whole companies of white-trash, clean for the first time in their lives, and bands of black niggers in white

robes. . . . And bringing up the end of the procession was a tribe of people whom she recognized at once as those who, like herself . . . had always had a little of everything and the God-given wit to use it right. . . . They alone were on key. Yet she could see by their shocked and altered faces that even their virtues were being burned away.

Here O'Connor uses a vision as an epiphany, in the true religious sense of the word, as Mrs. Turpin quite literally sees the light for the first time.

Often a short story or novel that makes use of frequent flashbacks, dreams, or visions takes on a structure like a dolphin swimming, alternating time spent at the surface, the story's present, with fluid dives into the past, the future, or the subconscious of the dream world. Remember that the last flashback, vision, or dream is always the most telling because of its position in the story. This is true even if the first flashback is of a character's father dying and the last of a poodle getting run over—true even if the father's death is a dream and the poodle's a vision of a future occurrence. The poodle's death gains weight from its place in the story, which signals readers that this death is something the character is more reluctant to reveal and therefore more important to the resolution of the internal conflict.

When using flashbacks, visions, and dreams, be careful where you leave a character physically (standing, sitting, falling from an airplane) while he is having these mental experiences. While readers are off in the past, the future, or some alternate reality with your character, he is left in the story's present in the readers' minds. This is fine if your character is driving down Interstate 5 to a funeral. You can just leave him rolling down a nice straight road while he remembers how his mother used to bake him cupcakes or beat the living daylights out of him, but if he is careening down a treacherous mountain road or in the middle of a tire iron fight at a truck stop, readers are more likely to feel an urgent need to return to the story's present. A good rule of thumb is that a character can have a longer flashback in the bathtub than in the shower.

A final warning about this category of thoughts: Not every story needs flashbacks, visions, or dreams. Sometimes the story is overwhelmingly about the here and now. In this case, whatever past information we need about the characters and their conflicts should be brought out through direct action or dialogue. Let's say our character isn't alone on his long drive to his mother's funeral but has his estranged older brother in the Chevy with him. If the point of the story is to make him face his brother for the first time in years, then perhaps we don't want to let him out of the car, even by way of his thoughts. But a good flashback, dream, or vision, well told, aptly timed and placed, is often the very thing that makes a character and a story come alive for readers. Aha, they say. Now we understand.

FOUR HINTS FOR HOLDING YOUR READER

You don't want to concentrate on the framework of your conflicts to the exclusion of allowing room for the rich detail that will make those conflicts seem real and involving. Let me end this chapter by suggesting four other strategies that can add interest, even piquancy, to a short story or novel.

1. Readers like to learn when they read, even when they are reading fiction. If you know a good deal about anything (collecting antiques, crewing a shrimp boat, working in an emergency room), consider putting some of this knowledge into the story. You can do this by giving your background to one of the characters or by using it as a part of the conflict (a divorced couple bidding on the same oak table at an antique auction). If you want to include some authentic and interesting details in a story but don't know a darn thing about shrimping, hit the library or ask a friend. There is a general suspicion among fiction writers that all the interesting things in life happen to other people. If you feel nothing interesting has ever happened to you (though I can assure you this is not the case), get your running partner to tell you what it was like working the Alaskan Pipeline. Within reason this kind of background material is fair game.

2. As the mantra of the 1960s went, wherever you go, there you are. Setting is another pleasure important to your fiction. It helps to think of place as another character. In some fiction the setting may be a central character (Flannery O'Connor's rural South or Anne Tyler's Baltimore). In others, such as Ann Beattie's short stories, it may play a minor role. All stories are set somewhere, so it might as well be an interesting somewhere. Think about all the places you know. Where did you grow up? Where do you live now? Where have you traveled?

I have set stories in Florida (where I grew up) and in towns like Iowa City (where I once lived) and in other places like St. Louis and Kansas City (where I briefly visited). My novel, *The Museum of Happiness*, which is partly set in Paris, taught me a great lesson about the power of place. Half the comments I have heard from readers are about how much they loved reading about Paris, a city they had (a) visited often and missed or (b) never visited but always wanted to.

3. Readers appreciate familiar things, sharply observed. Some authors specialize in a sharp satirical eye, others in making the ordinary memorable and extraordinary. Take some common experience (going to the dentist, eating a hot dog) and describe it lovingly or wittily, but in either case with great care.

4. A short story or novel can nearly always benefit from one detail or event that is both unusual and memorable. I don't mean that someone has to be gunned down (in fiction and increasingly in life, this is neither unusual nor memorable). From the large (Moby Dick, the world's only white whale) to the small (Ed Wolfe throwing all the money he has in the world into the air), every story can benefit from having something in it readers have never quite seen before, something that an editor, after reading your work, finds she just can't forget and, we writers all pray, that she simply must publish.

EXERCISES

1. Review the list of ten trips that you made in chapter one. Pick one and write a scene using a first-person narrator or third-person point-of-view character. Establish the external conflict by making clear who is going where on this trip and why. Then advance the external conflict by complicating the journey.

2. Next add or heighten internal conflict in this scene by using each of the two methods we've discussed: thoughts about the current situation and thoughts about another time (flashbacks or dreams or visions).

3. Write a brief account of a typical day in the life of a character very like someone you know (day in the life of a housewife, college student, tax accountant).

4. Now heighten the internal conflict in the typical day by using thoughts, flashbacks, dreams, or visions.

5. Number a page from one to thirty and write a chapter outline for

an imaginary Bildungsroman that would cover the childhood, coming-of-age, and early adulthood of a character. The first chapter should be "Chapter One: I Was Born."

6. Write a scene from a third-person point of view placing a flashback in the middle.

7. Make a list of your peculiar and specialized bits of knowledge (as in I know how to do CPR, grow prize-winning African violets, sell crack). Write a scene in which you weave in very specific information readers aren't likely to know (the proper way to gut a catfish or to assemble a Burger King Whopper).

CHAPTER EIGHT

ENDINGS IN FICTION

When editors send back a short story or reject a novel, nine times out of ten they will say the ending didn't work for them. In workshops the first point students make about another student's short story is that the ending didn't quite work. As a writer I've developed an allergy to hearing the words *didn't work* and *ending* together. Be original, I want to say to a rejection note or a critical review, tell me the middle didn't work for you. Part of the criticism endings catch is inherently unfair. If a story hasn't been working all along, the conclusion is unlikely to save it. It becomes the fall guy.

Still, every reader and editor does have the right to complain about a less than satisfying ending, just as all home buyers have every right to refuse to accept a home as finished that still has no shingles. For better or worse, your closing caps your story the way a roof does a house. It is the last thing an editor or your readers see, and last impressions, like first ones, count heavily in fiction.

As you know, the end must bring about the resolution of both the external and internal conflicts, and, beyond that, it must combine the inevitable with the surprising. It must be inevitable because readers have lived with the conflicts through all their ups and downs and want them resolved; it must be surprising because the conflicts should be solved in a way readers cannot entirely have foreseen. Readers who put down their books, saying in disgust, "I knew it would end like that," are unlikely to become lifelong fans.

INTERNAL CONFLICTS

There are as many possible internal conflicts as there are people and desires in the world. If you are unsure what a character can want badly, a quick look at the Ten Commandments or a list of the seven deadly sins will give you a few ideas. Buddhist tradition is also full of lists of earthly desires that ensnare men and keep them from achieving nirvana. Most of us are human enough to know about desire without extensive research. Whatever the yearning, the formula for internal conflict remains that your character wants something and keeps himself from getting it. This bit of masochism may not be intended or conscious. Very often it is the character's own doubts or lack of self-knowledge that keep satisfaction at bay. Though there are a multitude of possible conflicts, there are really only two endings possible to an internal conflict: a character can either *come to realize* or *fail to realize*.

Comes to Realize

This is by far the most common conclusion to internal conflict. In David Leavitt's short story "Territory," Neil, a young gay man, brings his lover home to meet his mother. Throughout the story it is touch-and-go whether Neil can bring himself to separate enough from his mother to make a life with Wayne. On the plane on the way home, Wayne takes Neil's hand.

> For a moment, Neil wonders what the stewardess or the old woman on the way to the bathroom will think, but then he laughs and relaxes.
>
> Later, the plane makes a slow circle over New York City, and on it two men hold hands, eyes closed, and breathe in unison.

Wayne is offering love. Neil has to decide whether to accept it, in the same way Cinderella has to decide to put her foot in the glass slipper: "For a moment, Neil wonders what the stewardess or the old woman on the way to the bathroom will think." Neil hesitates, but then leaves his hand in Wayne's. Neil has come to realize that being with Wayne is more important than what people think, that for him it is the most important thing in the world. Cinderella decides she deserves love, sticks her foot in that slipper, and she and the prince marry. If you want your characters to live happily ever after, they need, like Neil, to realize at some level what it is that keeps them from being happy and either change or at least realize change is possible.

As is so often the case with short stories, Neil's realization takes place in the last few sentences. This is also true in Mary Robison's "Pretty Ice." This brief short story opens with the practical narrator and her seemingly misguided and overcheerful mother headed to the train station to meet the younger woman's fiancé, Will, whom she has not seen in some time. The narrator wants to be happy but doesn't know how to be and hopes against hope that Will is the answer. On the way to the station, we have time to learn Will, a grass taxonomist, has just had his work dismissed as superficial and lost his research grant. When the fiancé finally appears and the narrator sees him, she is disappointed and knows her mother is too.

> He seemed to have put on weight, girlishly, through the
> hips, and his face looked thicker to me, from temple to temple.
> His gold-rimmed spectacles looked too small.

Will seems pedantic and old. He seems to have even less hope for the future than the narrator. There has been an ice storm, and the sun is glinting off the frozen branches of the maples and the buckeye trees.

> "It's twinkling like a stage set," Mother said.
> "It is pretty," I said.
> Will said, "It'll make a bad-looking spring. A lot of shrubs
> get damaged. . . ."
> For once I agreed with my mother. Everything was quiet
> and holding still. Everything was in place, the way it was sup-
> posed to be. I put my comb away and smiled back at Will—
> because I knew it was for the last time.

The internal crisis starts at the line "For once I agreed with my mother. Everything was quiet and holding still. Everything was in place, the way it was supposed to be." She has come to realize her happiness is in her own hands. Her smile is the crisis action. The story's resolution is the half line "because I knew it was for the last time." Will is not her prince. Your characters can realize they were wrong about what they wanted. One could be the Cinderella who realizes what she really wants to do is run away and join the circus. Another could be the prince who gives up his throne and goes to medical school.

Just because the internal conflict ends with a character coming to realize does not mean the story has a happy ending. In Flannery O'Connor's "A Good Man Is Hard to Find," a grandmother, her son, his wife, and their two children set out on a vacation to Florida in spite of the grandmother's strenuous objections. But they never get there. The grandmother talks her son into a detour in search of a half-remembered plantation house, and they are ambushed in the woods by a criminal called the Misfit. All of the members of the family except the grandmother are led into the woods and shot. She stays with the Misfit, who tells her why he believes there is "no pleasure but meanness" and that he wishes he had been present to see one of Christ's miracles because "if I had of been there I would of known and I wouldn't be like I am now." The grandmother has a sudden, unexpected vision.

> His voice seemed about to crack and the grandmother's head cleared for an instant. She saw the man's face twisted close to her own as if he were going to cry and she murmured, "Why, you're one of my babies. You're one of my own children!" She reached out and touched him on the shoulder. The Misfit sprang back as if a snake had bitten him and shot her three times through the chest.

The grandmother's realization may save her soul, but it does not save her life.

Fails to Realize

The second possible resolution to internal conflict is one in which the character fails to realize something. Usually this involves tiptoeing to the very edge of realization only to pull back or turn away from self-knowledge and the possibility of change. This is true in noted African-American author Charles Johnson's short story "Exchange Value." The narrator and his brother Loftis break into the apartment of Miss Bailey, a crazy elderly neighbor now mysteriously missing, who has spent her life hoarding anything she can get her hands on, including five Maxwell House Coffee cans full of human feces,

> glass jars of pennies, a set of bagpipes, an almost complete Model A Ford dappled with rust, and, I swear, three sections of a dead tree.

There is $879,543 in cash, the bulk of which was left to her by her former employer as a reward for her twenty years of service as a maid. The brothers also find the missing woman dead and rotting in her bed, surrounded by all her possessions and unspent wealth. One brother asks the other why Miss Bailey didn't just spend the money. The question seems to mesmerize Loftis, who declares, "The instant you buy something, you *lose* the power to buy something."

When the narrator finds a penny his brother has brought home and it is wrapped in a piece of paper on which he has written when and where he found it, he knows that his brother—and, by extension, he himself—is going to end up like Miss Bailey, dead in bed and surrounded by unspent wealth. He wants to tell Loftis to resist.

> Me, I wanted to tell Loftis how Miss Bailey looked four days ago, that maybe it didn't have to be like that for us—did it?—because we could change. Couldn't we?

The storyteller stands poised on the verge of speaking the truth that will save his brother, or at least himself, but he turns away. He does not speak. Instead he says,

> I . . . wrap up the penny, and, when I locate Miss Bailey's glass jar in the livingroom, put it away carefully, for now, with the rest of our things.

He refuses to realize, and so seals their fate. If you want your story to conclude on a poignant note, having your character come close to happiness can be very effective. Readers see clearly what the character should do, so when he doesn't do it, they feel the loss doubly.

Sometimes the central character in a novel or short story is so resistant to realization that the resolution to the internal conflict can be said to take place partly in readers' minds, not the character's. This is often the case in fiction where satire or social commentary is the main point. In a novel like British author Anthony Burgess' controversial *A Clockwork Orange,* any change of heart the narrator Alex experiences is not as important as our growing realization of how much Burgess' ugly dystopia resembles our own violent time, and how much more we have in common with the reprehensible Alex than we would originally have been willing to admit.

This is true as well in Stanley Elkin's short story "A Poetics for Bullies." In the first sentence, the speaker announces himself.

> I'm Push the bully, and what I hate are new kids and sissies, dumb kids and smart, rich kids, poor kids, kids who wear glasses, talk funny, . . . and cripples, *especially* cripples. I love nobody loved.

Push's power over the neighborhood kids is broken by the arrival of a new kid, John Williams, who is not only perfect himself, but improves everyone, urging the fat kids to lose weight, helping the dim ones to study. He wants to help Push, too, coming to his house and calling, "Please open the door, Push. . . . I think I can help you be happier."

Push could be said to be a classic case of fails-to-realize. He doesn't accept that John Williams is probably right. Push stubbornly clings to his role as bully, saying, "I may be wrong. I am probably wrong. All I know at last is what feels good." By this time readers, too, are a bit tired of John Williams' perfection and may find that as Push fights back, they are rooting for the bully to win. Elkin's title, after all, is "A Poetics for Bullies," and Push takes his calling to the highest, most uncompromising level, the level of art. The story ends with his declaration,

> I will not be reconciled, or halve my hate. It's what I have, all I can keep. . . . I force them off. I press them, thrust them aside. *I push through.*

If your main reason for writing a short story or novel is to make a larger political or philosophical point or to challenge your readers' conceptions of themselves, then having an unlikable central character who refuses to realize, refuses to change, may be just the approach you need to make your case in a way readers can't ignore.

EXTERNAL CONFLICTS

Remember that the conclusion to the external conflict is always a visible crisis action. In short stories this action is often quite small. Sometimes it involves a symbolic object such as Cinderella's slipper, sometimes it is merely a meaningful gesture. In novels a larger event is often required to serve as a convincing crisis action. First though, let's examine the two categories of small crisis actions: objects and gestures. Then we'll talk about larger, more novelistic endings.

Symbolic Objects

In Charles Johnson's short story "Exchange Value," the symbolic object in the crisis action is the wrapped penny the narrator puts "away carefully, for now, with the rest of our things" in one of the late Miss Bailey's jars. Since it is established from the beginning what hoarding means, the penny functions in this story just as neatly as the glass slipper in *Cinderella*. It clearly signals the brothers' fate, though their fate is not a happy one.

The trick to ending your story with a symbolic object, as Charles Johnson does with the fateful penny, is that you must establish its meaning earlier in the story. Remember when the slipper appears at the end of *Cinderella*, its meaning is already evident. Likewise the jars of pennies are introduced in an early description of Miss Bailey's mad possessions, and the deadly toll of her hoarding made abundantly clear, even though this particular coin doesn't appear until the end. If you find yourself cluttering your last lines with an explanation of what your symbolic object means, take it as a sure sign of trouble. Go back and work that all-important information into the body of your short story or novel. Then your finale will work, and the story will click shut like the well-made piece it is.

The object that closes a story need not always be small enough to fit in the palm of a hand or slip onto a dainty foot. In Stuart Dybek's award-winning short story "Hot Ice," the object is a girl frozen in ice. According to a neighborhood legend, the girl was a virgin who dove from a boat in the lake to escape the unwanted attention of two sailors. She drowned in the weeds near the shore, where her father found her, scooped her up, and ran with her in his arms, until he "reached the icehouse he owned, where crazy with grief he sealed her in ice."

Protagonist Eddie Kapusta, feeling trapped in his dying neighborhood, is obsessed with the legend, and finally he and a friend break into the icehouse, now scheduled for demolition. There they liberate a great block they believe holds the girl, wrestle it onto an old railroad handcar and push off.

    ... though Manny couldn't see the lake, he could feel it. ...
    he could recall the sudden lightness of freedom he'd felt once

> when he had speared out underwater and glided effortlessly
> away, one moment expanding into another. . . . He knew now
> where they were taking her, where she would finally be
> released. . . . Below, streetlights shimmered watery in the old
> industrial neighborhoods. Shiny with sweat, the girl already
> melting free between them, they forced themselves faster,
> rowing like a couple of sailors.

Manny's vision of the lake is the internal crisis, his moment of coming-to-realize. Pumping the handcar "like a couple of sailors" functions as the crisis action. The internal and external resolution work together, and for the first time in years, Manny and Eddie feel free.

If you want to resolve an internal conflict by having your character, like Manny and Eddie, experience a true epiphany, don't be afraid to let things get a bit strange. Dreams and visions often are. Remember Mrs. Turpin's vision at the end of Flannery O'Connor's "Revelation." If you need some additional examples of realistic descriptions of slightly unreal events, you may want to read the works of Nobel prize-winner Gabriel García Márquez or, better still, the Bible, a book in which epiphanies occur and angels appear to men on a regular basis.

Meaningful Gestures

At the end of short stories, even small gestures carry enough weight to serve as crisis actions. In David Leavitt's "Territory" after Wayne takes Neil's hand, Neil hesitates, "then he laughs and relaxes." The laughter is the crisis action, and this sentence leaves little doubt about our lovers' future together. Gestures, unlike symbolic objects, need not be established or introduced earlier in the story to work as crisis actions. Our reaction to Neil's laughter and his relaxing rests on our knowledge of human behavior. It is as if, instead of using the glass slipper, Cinderella took the prince's hand in hers. If you want to end your short story or novel on a quiet, human note, have one character reach out to another or turn away.

Sometimes the meaning of a closing gesture is more ambiguous, with both positive and negative reverberations. In T. Coraghessan Boyle's short story "Greasy Lake," the narrator tells the tale of when

> We were nineteen. We were bad. We read André Gide and
> struck elaborate poses to show that we didn't give a shit about
> anything. At night, we went up to Greasy Lake.

In the course of this particular night, the speaker and his two friends
find their suburban brand of badness put to the test. They flash their
lights at a car they believe belongs to a friend, hoping to catch him
with a girl, but the car belongs to a truly bad character. There is a
fight, and the narrator hits the bad guy with a tire iron. Then the three
boys almost turn truly bad themselves, very nearly raping the "fox"
who was in the car. But it turns out the bad guy isn't dead. In an
instant the boys turn from hunters to prey. The narrator escapes by
diving into the lake, accidently discovering a genuinely dead body.
He has to hide with it as he listens to the sound of his parents' car
being vandalized as an act of vengeance. Finally when the boys
emerge from their hiding places in the morning, another girl turns
up, stoned, and asks if they want to party.

> I just looked at her. I thought I was going to cry. . . .
> I put the car in gear and it inched forward with a groan,
> shaking off pellets of glass like an old dog shedding water
> after a bath. . . . There was a sheen of sun on the lake. I
> looked back. The girl was still standing there, watching us,
> her shoulder slumped, hand outstretched.

After his discovery of the body in the lake, the young man seems
to have lost all taste for wild adventures. He seems to have come to
realize he is not bad. He is praying to live long enough to forget the
night ever happened. One of his friends is letting his father pay his
way through Cornell, and it is easy to imagine a comfortable, suburban
future for the narrator as well after the shock of a night like this one.
The final gesture of the teenager looking back at the lake as the sun
comes up, his seeing the girl still standing there with hand out-
stretched, adds just the right touch of uncertainty. The boy may not
have ever been truly bad, but that life does call to him. The ambiguity
of the final gesture says maybe the suburbs and the good life are not
going to swallow him entirely.

If, like T. Coraghessan Boyle in "Greasy Lake," you want to close on a subtle or ambiguous note you can have your character do something that shows this open-endedness. If an unambiguous ending would be a character's opening a door (hope) or shutting one (despair), then a more subtle one would be having your character open the door but turn for one last longing look at the darkness he is leaving. Be careful, though, about sending unintentional mixed messages that seem to ask readers to choose which conclusion you intend. If you mean to leave a character in a state of despair, don't have her shut the window, then turn on a light.

Rites of Passage

Though external conflicts in short stories can often be resolved with relatively small crisis actions, sometimes in fiction a larger event is required for a sense of closure. This is particularly true with novels. The more time we spend with characters, the more settled we want their lives to be when we leave them. Mere gestures or the handling of symbolic objects won't do. We are drawn to rites of passage, such as death, marriage, and birth, or to significant events, such as leaving home or coming back again, to give a final shape to the stories of the characters' lives.

When Characters Die

Death, especially the death of a central character, is more common as a crisis action in a novel than a short story. This has to do with the more extended falling action and resolution the longer structure of the novel provides. When a character dies in the next-to-last chapter of a novel, there is still space for the surviving characters to sort out where the death leaves them and for readers to prepare to leave the characters they have devoted so much time to learning about. This is certainly true in nineteenth-century French writer Gustav Flaubert's classic novel *Madame Bovary*. The crisis action of the novel is Emma Bovary's decision to escape her troubles through suicide. She goes to the pharmacist's, talks her way past his assistant and goes after the poison.

> She went straight to the third shelf—so well did her memory serve her as guide—seized the blue jar, tore out the cork, plunged in her hand, withdrew it full of white powder, and ate greedily. . . .

> Then she went home, suddenly at peace—almost as serene
> as though she had done her duty.

Emma then dies slowly and horribly in her bed at home.

> Emma began to laugh—a horrible, frantic, desperate
> laugh—fancying that she saw the beggar's hideous face, a
> figure of terror looming up in the darkness of eternity. . . .
> A spasm flung her down on the mattress. Everyone drew
> close. She had ceased to exist.

In these scenes it is clear Emma has come to realize the truth of her situation. But like many novels, *Madame Bovary* has other point-of-view characters who must either realize or fail to realize, and so it continues for another three chapters, following the fates of the people in Emma's life. The night of her funeral, her lover, Rodolphe, whose refusal to lend her money precipitates her death, feels next to nothing, and her other lover, Léon, does not even know she is dead.

> Rodolphe, who had spent all day roaming the woods to
> keep his mind off things, was peacefully asleep in his chateau;
> and Léon was sleeping, too, in the distant city.

Rodolphe and Léon are left untouched by Emma's death. They do not realize. Only her long-suffering husband, Charles, is thinking ceaselessly of her, but he, too, is deluded. The last chapters chart the stages of his grief and his eventual discovery of the letters from Rodolphe and Léon. The first he passes off as platonic, and he continues to love Emma in death, planning a great monument for her grave marker. He even changes the way he dresses.

> To please her, as though she were still alive, he adopted
> her tastes, her ideas: he bought himself patent leather shoes,
> took to wearing white cravats. He waxed his mustache, and
> signed—just as she had—more promissory notes. She was
> corrupting him from beyond the grave.

When he discovers her letters to Léon, there can be no doubt of her infidelity, and with his realization he falls into a depression from which he never recovers. He dies, and all his possessions are seized. His daughter is forced to live with an aunt who sends her to work in a cotton mill.

If you plan for one of your main characters to die by her own hand or of natural causes, remember that readers are deeply concerned and expect to be there, step by step. As in *Madame Bovary*, this means writing scenes with the dying character and with surviving characters as they mourn her. Mrs. Ramsay, in Virginia Woolf's *To the Lighthouse*, dies between one page and the next with hardly a mention, but that is the exception in fiction. Usually readers are allowed access to the emotions of the characters involved in this ending of endings.

This is certainly the case in *Anna Karenina*, Leo Tolstoy's great Russian novel. Anna also kills herself over love's complications. At the train station, she remembers seeing a man run over the day she first met her lover, Count Vronsky, and knows what she must do. She throws herself under the moving train, experiencing a final realization as she does.

> "God forgive me everything!" she said, feeling the impossi-
> bility of struggling. . . . The candle, by the light of which she
> had been reading that book filled with anxieties, deceptions,
> grief, and evil, flared up with a brighter light than before, lit
> up for her all that had before been dark, flickered, began to
> grow dim, and went out for ever.

If this were a short story, it might very well end with those words, but Tolstoy, like Flaubert, allows time in the closing chapters for those who knew her to find answers for themselves to the meaning of her life.

Tragic death is not reserved for women alone (thank goodness), nor is it always the fate of a central point-of-view character or narrator. In F. Scott Fitzgerald's novel *The Great Gatsby*, Jay Gatsby doesn't step in front of a train or take poison, but his obsession with Daisy Buchanan and her actions lead directly to his murder. He knows full well what is coming, but, as the narrator Nick Carraway clearly sees, after his rejection and betrayal by Daisy, Gatsby no longer has the will to go on.

> Perhaps he no longer cared. If that was true he must have
> felt that he had lost the old warm world, paid a high price for
> living too long with a single dream. He must have looked up
> at an unfamiliar sky through frightening leaves and shivered
> as he found what a grotesque thing a rose is and how raw the

sunlight was upon the scarcely created grass. A new world, material without being real, where poor ghosts, breathing dreams like air, drifted fortuitously about . . . like that ashen, fantastic figure gliding toward him through the amorphous trees.

The chauffeur . . . heard the shots.

Gatsby dies, leaving Nick Carraway to do the book's summing up. Nick imagines the first night Gatsby realized he could pick out the green light on Daisy's dock across the water.

> Gatsby believed in the green light, the orgiastic future that year by year recedes before us. It eluded us then, but that's no matter—tomorrow we will run faster, stretch out our arms farther. . . . And one fine morning—
> We beat on, boats against the current, borne back cease-lessly into the past.

Gatsby is gone, but his death forever changes Nick, our guide to Gatsby's world.

One of the great appeals of death as an ending is that the demise of a single character can often stand for much more. Gatsby's death stands for the end of the Roaring Twenties in Prohibition America. In your novel or short story, if the grandfather who brought the family from Italy dies or the last cowboy working on the family's ranch passes, an era or a world has died too.

When Characters Marry

There is a long tradition of using marriage as a crisis action. After all Cinderella and the prince marry and live happily ever after. In recent years many women have come to doubt that one walk down the aisle, in a life statistically likely to include a career and several marriages, will be the high point of their lives. There is also a growing suspicion of marriage as a final act in serious fiction, though it is still the life's blood of the romance novel industry. Yet, it is probably too good an option for writers to surrender permanently. One sign of this may be the current revival of interest in the novels of Jane Austen, an author who perfected the pursuit of a proper marriage as a subject for fiction. Her early novel *Sense and Sensibility* sets the pattern. In it two sisters

overcome early misfortune and mistakes of judgment and tempera-
ment to marry well and live happily within sight of one another.

Marriages as crisis actions, however, are not always synonymous
with happy endings. Faulkner's dark comic masterpiece *As I Lay
Dying*, a book we noted earlier for its use of multiple points of view,
begins with a death. Most of the novel concerns the struggle of the
Bundren family to haul their mother Addie's dead body forty hard
miles to the town of Jefferson where her husband, Anse, promised
she would be buried. One son, Cash, is almost killed crossing the
river with the wagon; another, Darl, is sent away to the state mental
hospital after he burns down a barn trying to cremate his mother and
end the trip. Not one of the five children is left unscarred by the
time they reach Jefferson. But the conclusion of the novel isn't their
mother's burial which, indeed, is barely alluded to, but the moment
when their father, who has gone off with "his hair combed wet and
slick and smelling sweet with perfume," comes back wearing a new
set of false teeth and accompanied by a woman. Cash notices

> a kind of duck-shaped woman all dressed up, with them kind
> of hard-looking pop eyes like she was daring ere a man to say
> nothing. . . .
> "It's Cash and Jewel and Vardaman and Dewey Dell," pa
> says, kind of hangdog and proud too, with his teeth and all,
> even if he wouldn't look at us. "Meet Mrs Bundren," he says.

And so Addie, the first Mrs. Bundren, is both buried and replaced.
Mrs. Bundren is dead. Long live Mrs. Bundren. If your view or your
characters' view of marriage is less sanguine than Austen's, then you
may want to use bad, doomed, or even wicked marriage as a crisis
action.

When Characters Give Birth
The third rite of passage often used as a crisis action is one that
proceeds naturally from all the happy and unhappy marrying in fiction.
The birth of a child, that ultimate symbol of the renewal of life, can
give a satisfying sense of closure. My novel, *The Museum of Happiness*,
ends when Ginny is reunited with Roland, her lover, and gives birth
to their son. Just before Roland arrives, Ginny goes into premature
labor.

A foot. Ginny tried to remember what the procedures were for a breech birth, but the pain came back full force, and she couldn't think. If one foot was sticking out, then the crucial question was, where was the other foot? The baby had to get two feet out to be born. She thought she felt the wandering foot like a boot in her spine. Maybe, she thought, dizzy from panting, this baby doesn't want to be born.

The midwife gives Ginny gas and she feels herself floating out of her body, above Le Puy, the town where she is living, above France, out over the ocean and back to her home in Florida. In a vision she sees her mother, her father, her crazy Aunt Fanny. Only Roland's arrival brings her back, saves the baby and her life. The midwife holds the baby up for Ginny to see.

The baby thrashed its arms and legs, trying out the air. It had had no extra two months in the womb to rest and get wrinkled. Its skin was pink and smooth. . . .

Odile said, "It's a boy." . . .

But Ginny could have sworn she said, *What joy!*

If you use a birth as your crisis action, the ultimate meaning of the act is still in your hands, as was the case with death and marriage. No rite of passage you use as a crisis action is automatically sad or happy, positive or negative. You are the author, and through your characters' internal conflicts and realizations you control how readers respond to any crisis, large or small.

You Can/Can't Go Home Again

Homecomings and leave-takings are both traditional endings in fiction. In the previous chapter, we discussed journeys as natural sources of internal and external conflict. Leave-taking as crisis action is a variation on this structure, one where the trip doesn't begin until the end of the short story or novel, though the practical and psychological pressures that lead to the departure or return have usually been building throughout the story. This is certainly the case in Marilynne Robinson's wonderful novel *Housekeeping*. Ruth, the narrator, grows closer and closer to her fey, slightly mad Aunt Sylvie and more and more detached from school, the town, and reality. When the sheriff comes to take Ruth out of Sylvie's care, the two act.

> For we had to leave. I could not stay, and Sylvie would not stay without me. Now truly we were cast out to wander, and there was an end to housekeeping. Sylvie set fire to the straw of the broom, and held it blazing to the hem of the pantry curtain, and to the fringe of the rug, so there were two good fires, but then we heard a train whistle, and Sylvie said, "We have to run! Get your coat!" I did.

Clearly, there can be no return home for Ruth and Sylvie. For better or worse, they are launched into the wider world. If you want your character's leave-taking to make a convincing crisis action, you, too, may want to literally or symbolically burn that person's bridges.

A homecoming is a crisis action in which the hero or heroine, after a significant absence, returns in triumph or defeat to a place of importance. In Charlotte Brontë's *Jane Eyre* the crisis action is such a homecoming, Jane's return to Rochester. Like so many crisis actions in novels, this takes place in the next-to-last chapter.

> "Jane Eyre!—Jane Eyre!" was all he said.
>
> "My dear master," I answered, "I am Jane Eyre: I have found you out—I am come back to you."
>
> "In truth?—in the flesh? My living Jane?"
>
> "You touch me, sir—you hold me, and fast enough: I am not cold like a corpse, nor vacant like air, am I?"
>
> ". . . It is a dream; such dreams as I have had at night when I have clasped her once more to my heart . . . and trusted that she would not leave me."
>
> "Which I never will, sir, from this day."

Jane had left in disgrace and confusion a year before, but now returns rich and committed to helping the love of her life regain his sight and his spirit. This leaves their wedding and their living happily ever after for the falling action of the last chapter.

Sometimes journeys are more metaphorical, and in this case the crisis action might be as well. Amy Tan's short story "The Joy Luck Club," which she later expanded into the novel of the same title, opens with a request the father makes of the narrator, a request that establishes the story's internal and external conflicts.

> My father has asked me to be the fourth corner at the Joy
> Luck Club. I am to replace my mother, whose seat at the mah
> jong table has been empty since she died two months ago.

The young woman feels inadequate taking her mother's place in such an intensely Chinese setting. She remembers her mother saying she was going to make a special soup for the women in the club, one even better than the black sesame-seed soup served by the previous hostess.

> "Don't show off," I said.
> "It's not showoff." She said the two soups were almost the same, *chabudwo*. Or maybe she said *butong*, not the same thing at all. . . . I can never remember things I didn't under-stand in the first place.

But after recalling the stories her mother told her about her life in China and her experiences in coming to America, the narrator is ready to take her place at the table, to join the Joy Luck Club, to come home. And so the short story ends with the daughter's acceptance of her father's request, "And I am sitting at my mother's place at the mah jong table, on the East, where things begin."

If you are thinking about using a real or symbolic homecoming as your crisis action, the important point to remember is to establish what or where home is. In this sense, it is like any other symbol, like Cinderella's slipper or the found penny in "Exchange Value."

THE LIVING END

The perfect ending resolves the already established interior and exterior conflicts:

- the interior, by having the narrator or central point-of-view character either come to realize or fail to realize the truth of his situation
- the exterior, by using a small gesture, symbolic object, or a larger rite of passage as a crisis action

I should say here that when a short story or novel is really flowing, really working for me, all of this happens on an unconscious rather than a conscious level. I pick a final image or action by the way it feels, almost as if I had my eyes closed, reaching into a treasure chest to choose one magic jewel. At least this is the way I work on a first draft. If it turns out that my perfect jewel of an ending does nothing for readers, then I turn analytical and begin to revise, an all-important process covered in the next chapter. Most of the time, I find I can trust my instincts.

This way of thinking is quite different from the way critics approach an already finished work. I will always remember a dinner I had with the chair of the English department where I teach and another colleague. It was shortly after my first book, *The Dogeater*, was published. They had both read my short story "A Clean House." In it the narrator, Harriet Gundy, a widow whose health is rapidly failing, takes in a young woman, Jean, as housekeeper and nurse who gradually encourages Harriet to let go of all her cares and accumulated possessions. In some ways this is an entirely necessary and normal thing for Harriet to do. She is dying, and she needs to learn to say good-bye and let go. But Jean, it turns out, may be mad. She seems unable to feel pain, barely eats or drinks, and her encouragement of Harriet's increasing detachment has some of the overtones of a suicide pact. The story concludes with Harriet in bed dying, watched over by Jean. Jean tells her not to be sad or worried. "We go," she says, "then we stop. . . . That's not so bad, is it?" Harriet takes Jean's hand.

> She felt the apartment around her more transparent than glass now, like some soft permeable membrane with light and life moving through it as easily as air. . . . It was snowing. The white flakes blew up past the window into the white sky. As her eyes followed them upward, she felt so light herself that if Jean hadn't been holding her hand whatever was driving the snow upward would have drawn her up too. . . .
>
> "No," Harriet said, letting a breath go. "It doesn't seem bad at all."

Over wine and pasta, my two colleagues argued fiercely about whether the closing description of snow was a birth or a death image. The department chair said, "Snow is *always* death." My other companion disagreed. "It's blowing up," he said. "That makes it birth, or at least rebirth." They looked at me. I didn't know what to say. On a practical level, I knew I had chosen the closing image because as a Floridian recently moved to the wintery Midwest, I had been fascinated the first time I saw snow falling not down, but up. I sensed that under all the talk of symbolism they were really trying to decide if the story had a happy ending. What were we supposed to feel about Harriet's acceptance of death? All I could say was that I had felt the image of the snow blowing up past the window was the right one, one that had the same ambiguity, the same mixture of white as both purity and sterility, life and death, as the rest of the images in the story. My colleagues were looking at me, expecting a simpler answer.

I shrugged and hedged my bets. "A little birth," I said. "A little death." A writer's answer. They shook their heads.

EXERCISES

1. Take an idea from your list of Potential Story Ideas or a story you have already started and write an ending for it in which the narrator or point-of-view character comes to a realization that solves her internal conflict.

2. Rewrite your ending so the person fails to realize.

3. Take an idea from your list of Potential Story Ideas or a story you have already started and write a conclusion for it in which the external conflict is resolved by an object.

4. Rewrite the ending so the external conflict is resolved with a gesture.

5. Write a scene that contains the crisis action for an imaginary novel in which a third-person point-of-view character dies, gets married, or has a child.

6. Write a scene that contains the crisis action to a short story or novel in which the character either leaves home or returns home.

CHAPTER NINE

REVISION

Most serious writers believe revision is what separates real writers from those who only think they want to write, the dedicated and talented from the merely talented. When I was at the Iowa Writers' Workshop, we fiction writers liked to think of ourselves as craftsmen, not because we didn't think we were artists, but because the word *craftsmen* implied long hours of painstaking work by people who really knew what they were doing.

This was partly defensive. The poets, our opposite numbers in that particular little world, always seemed to dress better, have wilder parties, and really know how to dance. We suspected them of living on pure inspiration, the poems effortlessly flowing out of their pens five minutes before class. So we took a perverse pride in the hours we spent hunched over word processors and typewriters. Some fiction writers even kept track of the number of drafts they put a short story through, the way a weight lifter counts reps. Revision was a cult of masochism, and we took pride in self-imposed pain of the kind that keeps athletes reciting the mantra *no pain, no gain*.

That is the wrong way to look at revision. Most writers who have been at it awhile will tell you with a straight face that revision is their favorite part of the writing process, and they mean it. They see revision as a time when the hard work of raising the framework and getting the roof on the story is done, and they can take pleasure in the finish work, the cabinetry and decorative details that make reading a pleasure.

Bernard Malamud said, "Revision is one of the true pleasures of writing." Whether you learn to love revision or dread it with the intensity most people reserve for trips to the dentist, all fiction deserving of the time and effort it took to write it in the first place also deserves careful, serious, and thorough revision.

In some ways it's an artificial distinction to think of revision as a separate stage in the writing process. When I am writing a short story or chapter, I am revising all the time. I write a sentence, glance back, and change a word or two. Write a paragraph, look it over, and cut a line or add one. My usual method is to write my way as far into a story as I can, stretching for the end. Inevitably I get stopped at some point by what I don't know or pulled back by the mistakes that have accumulated behind me. I may have discovered in writing the story that I need to tell it from a different point of view or that I want to turn a character from a landlord into a landlady. So I go back and make changes. Then I start forward again. The process is circular rather than linear. Sometimes I imagine my writing self as an old hound dog turning around and around before lying down.

There comes a stage, however, when I have made it through to what I hope is the perfect end to a perfect story. I allow myself to sigh with happiness, to sit for a moment awash in the golden glow of my successfully completed work. Then I come back to reality, and the real process of revision begins.

THE RHYTHM OF REVISION

The rhythm of revision is rather like marching: left brain, right brain, left brain, right brain. Your critical sense alternates with your creative sense. You assess the work with a cold eye, then reenter the creative world where all things are possible. It's important to learn to make these transitions. If you can't look at your work critically, you will be stuck forever with half-realized first drafts. If the pure unedited flow of thought and language is your only goal, keep a diary. If you keep it long enough and live in interesting times, you may earn a place in literary history without ever revising or publishing a word. This is what happened to the great diarist Samuel Pepys, chronicler of English life in the seventeenth century. At least you would leave a record of your life for your children and grandchildren. However, most writers aim for a larger audience, one that will read their work in their own lifetimes.

On the other hand, if you do not learn to separate the critical from the creative, you are setting the stage for an inevitable case of writer's block. If every time you look at a word, a line of dialogue, or a transition in a rough draft, you think, *This is crap*, and cross it out, you will never be able to finish, let alone publish, anything. When you are in the creative mode, you have to give yourself room to discover what it is you want to say even if it means giving yourself a license to write badly until you do.

THE CRITICAL EYE

When I finish a draft, I read it with a cold, hard eye, trying to see the story as it actually exists. This can be a discouraging experience. The stories on the pages never match the perfection of the ones in our heads. The trick at this stage is to remember we get to fix our mistakes, to bring the work closer and closer to our ideals. To do that we have to be rather ruthless in diagnosing what is working and what isn't.

All writers have their own quirks when it comes to the stages of writing, and revision is no exception. My own habits have changed over time. When I began I wrote drafts longhand on legal pads and typed the finished stories. Eventually I graduated to typing first drafts, and now I work on a computer. In addition to these technological changes, my approach varies from story to story and novel to novel. Still when I have completed a draft, I print out a clean copy and read it from beginning to end. I read it through at least once without marking anything. If I had a pen in one hand I would spend all my time marking typos and misplaced commas and not enough time asking myself the important question, *Does this story work?*

If it works well enough, I take the story and find a few good readers for their sage, or at least honest, advice. Even after all the years I have been writing, I find it hard to conduct a completely dispassionate and thorough exam myself (doctors are rarely capable of operating on themselves). Like most writers I have cultivated a small group of first readers, people who will take the time and care to give me useful and detailed responses, people who have a good sense of what my fiction tries to do.

Even in a room filled with writers, however, how do you know whose advice is good advice? Even very good writers can be poor critics. If someone praises your style and wit, the comments will seem brilliant. If she criticizes your flat characters and dull prose, the great temptation is to dismiss her as all wrong. But good writers learn to take a deep breath and think again. While their work is being discussed, I encourage my students to clear their minds, think Zen, and listen to what's being said. Imagine your critics are on the other side of a one-way mirror, I say. Pretend your story is a new snack food and you have paid these experienced snack food eaters to taste your product and tell you what they honestly think. Be quiet, let them talk, and take notes. If you waste your time and mental energy defending yourself, you will inhibit them from saying what they really think, and you will not be able to hear them anyway. If you can do it graciously, ask a few questions at the end if you don't understand quite what you are being told. Then go off and think about what's been said.

Not all criticism is valid. Even worse, not all of it is useful. Some of it will be silly, the result of sloppy reading. (These are people you won't be coming back to for more response.) Some is wonderful advice but for another story. Writers have a tendency to want all fiction to resemble their own. An experimental writer might ask you to make a story more experimental, and a more traditional writer to make your story less offbeat. Also readers bring their own interests to a story. Some might want a story to be about the father instead of the mother, but if that is not the story you want to write, it is not advice you can take. Usually good advice echoes doubts you had already. Good critics have a way of sticking their fingers right in those soft spots you hoped no one would notice. The best criticism is very specific. General complaints, like, "Gee, I just got bored after a while," are hard to respond to. A good critic will point to the place in a story where a scene or a stretch of dialogue went on half a page too long. Readers are also great for spotting a minor confusion that you had no idea was a problem, such as the names *Tim* and *Tom*, characters they couldn't keep straight. That's easy to fix: *Tim* and *Alfonse*.

If you find a writer in a workshop or a friend whose criticism is thorough and helpful, take that person to dinner, stay in touch. This is how you build a network of reliable first readers.

MAJOR REVISION

Whether you are the critic, reading your own work with an analytical eye, or someone else is, all criticism breaks down into two categories:

1. Problems of a larger structural nature that may require serious rethinking before you know what to do to fix them
2. Smaller problems that show up line by line and word by word, the sort that can usually be marked on the story itself

Both are important and connected. If you look only at the smaller issues, you risk not seeing the forest for the trees. It's like worrying about wallpaper when the wall itself is about to fall down, or rearranging furniture when the real problem is a gaping hole in the floor. You could struggle trying to get a line of dialogue right, not realizing that you don't know what the character should say because you don't know what she wants. Instead you should first establish her external and internal conflicts more clearly. On the other hand, if you only look at the story from a distance, only at the forest and not at the trees, you risk losing sight of the place on the page where the larger actions happen. A conflict that's muddy now could be made clear by a single good line of dialogue. A story is not made up of abstractions but of words, the very leaves on the trees.

Still it's best to consider the major renovations that need to be done (the macro questions) before dealing with minor remodeling (the micro questions). Over the years I've developed revision checklists for these two categories. I use them on every piece of fiction I finish.

Macro Revision Checklist
1. Check your external conflict.
- Does the story have an immediate and gripping external conflict?
- Does the external conflict keep tension alive throughout the story?
- If the first external conflict is resolved and its place taken by successive external conflicts, check each for conflict, crisis, and resolution to ensure that the parts are working.
- Is there a final crisis action bringing all the outstanding external conflicts together as the glass slipper fitting does in *Cinderella*?
- If there is more than one final crisis action (Cinderella puts her foot in the slipper and then takes it out), you are divided about how the story should end. Decide now.

2. Check your internal conflict.
- Is the internal conflict well established after one page of the short story or one chapter of the novel?
- Trace the internal conflict as it heats up and cools down throughout the story to make sure the flame doesn't burn out.
- When the internal conflict is finally resolved, do you use a dream or an image, or the character's thoughts and memories to make the moment significant and convincing?
- Which type of resolution is it, comes-to-realize or fails-to-realize? Decide now.

3. Check your point of view. If you are having trouble with developing external and internal conflicts, you may have chosen the wrong viewpoint.
- Is your third-person point-of-view character or first-person narrator well situated to tell the story either by participation or observation in the central conflict?
- Does your point-of-view character have the personality and skills to be an effective storyteller? Shyness, stupidity, inexperience, or dishonesty may make the character unsuitable for the job, although using a third-person authorial voice can overcome these problems.
- If you're using first person, check the effectiveness and consistency of the narrator's voice by comparing how it sounds in the first paragraph and the last. It must seem like the same person.
- If you're using third person, check the effectiveness of your use of the point-of-view character's thoughts, especially at critical moments like the resolution of the internal conflict.
- If you're using an authorial voice, is it effective or even necessary?
- If you're using a single narrator or point-of-view character, could you tell the story better with more?
- If you're using multiple points of view, could you tell the story better with fewer?

4. Check your characters.
- If readers don't understand your central character, but you're certain you're using the right point of view, see if you can put

more of the character on the page by adding action, thought, dialogue, and memories.

- If other major characters seem flat and underdeveloped, be sure that each has an internal conflict.
- If a character seems enigmatic, try putting her in a scene with others to draw out her personality and motivations.
- Check the development of your minor characters. They can lack internal conflict, but they should be clearly and vividly drawn.
- Count lines to see if the space the characters take up is proportional to their importance in the story.
- If a character has become too good for a minor role, make him more important. If he is superfluous, cut him entirely.
- If the story seems depopulated, add more characters.

5. Check your opening.
- Cut the first paragraph, page, or chapter to see if the story can stand without it. If it can, cut it.
- If you moved a scene from the middle to the beginning, or if you moved the end to the beginning, would it make a better opening than the one you have now?

6. Check your ending.
- If you removed the last paragraph, page, or chapter, would it make a difference? If not, cut.
- If the story continued for another paragraph, page, or chapter, would something happen to resolve the conflict more thoroughly, interestingly, or beautifully?

REVISION

After you and perhaps others have turned critical eyes on your poor, naked piece of fiction and it's been run through the mill of my Macro Revision Checklist, what comes next? You may have a pile of notes and a marked copy or two of your first draft. Looking over the accumulated evidence of your doubts and your readers' complaints, you may be tempted to just give up. At this stage it often seems easier to start another short story or another novel than to deal with the mess this one has turned out to be. A new idea may start glowing in the back of your mind, the proverbial grass that is always greener. Take a deep breath, and know that all fiction and all great writers have passed this way before. Read your notes and comments, and then take a hot bath or a long walk or make a huge batch of lentil soup. While your hands and body are occupied, count on your mind and your imagination to start back to work. Mull it over. (If there is a problem with that first scene, I could . . . and maybe the ending would work better if . . .)

The important thing now is to *stop* being critical and to start letting your creative self take over and come up with the solutions to the problems your analytical self discovered. If you say, *Forget it, that will never work*, your story is going to stay in pieces. If you go back to the story while still in a negative mood, cutting and adding and half-heartedly patching it together using the criticism you've received, you will end up with a story with as many ugly, highly visible scars as Frankenstein's creature. Nothing is more discouraging to me as a writer, an editor, or a teacher than to reread a story I critiqued and find that revision has made it worse. The writer has surrendered his story, given up his vision for it, his hope of perfecting it, and that is a sad, sickening sight.

You have to get back into the story and remember the dream that made you want to write it in the first place. I think of this stage as *re-vision*. You need to re-see your work with fresh eyes. It is easy for someone to suggest cuts, but only you can dream up wonderful new scenes, characters, conflicts, and images that were not there before. My students groan when I point to a spot in a story that I think needs something and I say, "Right here, add something brilliant." But really, that is all anyone can say to the author in the end. Go, be brilliant. I know you can do it. And you can.

LIFE IS REVISION

When I finished a first draft of my novel, *The Museum of Happiness*, I read it from start to finish and fell quite thoroughly out of love with it. The draft was told completely from Ginny's point of view, the American in Paris. Seen only through Ginny's inexperienced and foreign eyes, Roland, the other major character, didn't make sense. There was just too much Ginny couldn't know about Roland, his family, and his past. In other words, I checked my point of view (number three on my Macro Revision Checklist) and found that it did not work.

I decided to tell the story again, this time from Roland's point of view, intercutting these new chapters with the ones I had already written. It was a big decision. It meant writing hundreds of new pages, essentially writing a second book, but it worked. The novel became what I had dreamed it could be. It took the analytical half of my writing brain to realize the novel didn't work as it stood. But it took re-vision by my creative half to see how the problem could be fixed and get excited enough to plunge back in and do the work.

An excellent example of this kind of major revision can be found in a comparison of Raymond Carver's short story "The Bath," which appeared in his early collection *What We Talk About When We Talk About Love*, and "A Small, Good Thing," from his last collection, *Cathedral*. "A Small, Good Thing" is a revised version of "The Bath." Carver made changes in language from the original short story, but also larger, structural changes. Since both are published short stories, the usually private record of a writer's process of revision is there for all to see.

Both open with a mother ordering a birthday cake for her son. But the birthday boy is struck by a car, and though he walks home, something is clearly wrong. In "The Bath" the prose is more tightly controlled, the style more minimalist.

> The birthday boy told his mother what had happened. They
> sat together on the sofa. She held his hands in her lap. This
> is what she was doing when the boy pulled his hands away
> and lay down on his back.

In "A Small, Good Thing" the birthday boy has a name, and his mother a voice.

> But after the birthday boy was inside his house and was
> telling his mother about it, she sitting beside him on the sofa,
> holding his hands in her lap, saying, "Scotty, honey, are you
> sure you feel all right, baby?" thinking she would call the
> doctor anyway, he suddenly lay back on the sofa, closed his
> eyes, and went limp.

In both stories the boy remains in a coma at the hospital while the parents suffer in the waiting room anxious for word. In both, the baker, unaware of what has happened, keeps calling the house, angry the birthday cake hasn't been picked up. "The Bath" ends when the mother, momentarily home to take the bath in the title, answers the phone. A man's voice says, "It has to do with Scotty." Readers are left to wonder whether this last call is bad news from the hospital or the disgruntled baker calling yet again.

In "A Small, Good Thing," the boy dies suddenly of a hidden brain occlusion. The parents return home only to receive another call from the angry baker. The mother demands to be driven to the shopping center and confronts the baker working in his bakery in the middle of the night. When she tells him Scotty is dead, he clears a place for the parents to sit and insists they eat some of his hot rolls, saying, "You have to eat and keep going. Eating is a small, good thing in a time like this." The story ends with the baker and the parents talking and eating under fluorescent lights as bright as day. It is a very different ending from that of "The Bath," a more humane one, the work of an older, perhaps wiser, writer. And the product of revision.

MINOR REVISION

When you've finished the major revision, go through the items of the Macro Revision Checklist again just to make certain you haven't forgotten anything. If your short story or novel passes all the tests, it is in good shape in the ways that matter most. But your writing deserves attention to detail that goes even farther. Vladimir Nabokov was famous for writing each word on a separate index card so he could compose his sentences with exquisite and painstaking care. I have never done that in my revision, but I do apply the following steps to polish and shine my finished work.

I begin by slowly reading my short story or novel aloud to myself. Wherever something seems questionable in any way, I make a mark and continue reading. When I am done with the short story or have finished a chapter or two of the novel, I go back and move through word by word and sentence by sentence reworking the passages I marked and checking for the items below.

Micro Revision Checklist
1. Check your words.
   - If each word you used cost a dollar, could you find some your story didn't need?

- If you got paid by the word, what would you add to make your language denser, richer, more beautiful and effective?
- Jot down a list of words and phrases that you overuse, and weed them from your writing. The *find* or *search* function of a computer word processor makes this easy.
- Question any phrase that reminds you of something constantly repeated on television, in movies, or in books and magazines. Use your own language instead.

2. Check your descriptions.
   - If your characters were suspects in a robbery, would your readers be able to describe their ages, appearances, clothing, heights, weights, mannerisms, and attitudes to the police?
   - Is the physical setting for your story so consistent and believable and the relationship between different places so clear that you can sketch the floor plan of a house, the streets of a town, or the route of a cross-country trip that is important in your story? (Or at least so that the details of the setting aren't contradictory.)
   - Do you account for the time that passes, or do unexpected jumps, shifts, and discontinuities make your story hard to follow?

3. Check your dialogue.
   - Does each conversation do at least two of the following: advance the plot, develop the character who's speaking, help set the time and place?
   - Can you eliminate some unnecessary dialogue tags?
   - Can you insert some dialogue tags when it's unclear who's speaking?
   - Can you tell which characters are speaking from what they say?
   - Is the language characters use believable and consistent?
   - Do the characters breathe, cough, scratch, and in other ways act like human beings while they speak to each other?
   - Are your characters standing or sitting someplace while they speak, rather than floating in space?
   - Have you generated tension by having characters avoid speaking about what concerns them most, for example, arguing about their mother's lasagna recipe instead of her love?

4. Check your transitions.
   - If you move from one place to another, from one time to another, or from one character's consciousness to another, are the clues sufficient to keep readers from being confused?
   - Are you consistent in your use of paragraphing, extra white space, subheadings, chapter breaks, and other typographical signals of transition?

5. Check the first and the last, again.
   - Reread, polish, and primp your opening so that no readers will escape its attraction. (There is no catch if the fish doesn't take the bait.)
   - Reread, polish, and primp your ending. Endings of great stories and novels often have a heightened poetic quality about them that readers cannot forget. Is your language as good as your idea for the ending?

LETTING GO

At some point, revision must stop. Humans are not perfect, nor is the fiction they create. In his *Paris Review* interview, William Faulkner explains his view of our imperfectability.

> In my opinion, if I could write all my work again, I am convinced that I would do it better, which is the healthiest condition for an artist. That's why he keeps on working, trying again; he believes each time that this time he will do it, bring it off. Of course, he won't, which is why this condition is healthy. Once he did it, once he matched the work to the image, the dream, nothing would remain but to cut his throat, jump off the other side of that pinnacle of perfection into suicide.

One problem with writing on computers is that you can revise endlessly, change a word, change it back. It's easy to get stuck. You may spend precious and limited writing time fiddling with a line, paragraph, or chapter that you end up cutting later. When this happens to me, I force myself to move on. If I am writing new material, I set an egg timer and make myself write for twenty minutes without stopping or going back to revise. If I am revising, I try to leave questions I can't answer for the time being and move forward, trusting the creative half of my brain to keep working on the problem while my mind is elsewhere.

I may go through many drafts before I send a short story to a magazine. I might edit again before it appears in print. I might revise before it appears in a book of stories, but at some point I have to call a halt, and you will too. If you don't, you risk revising a single short story or novel into the many other ones you might have written. Start a novel when you are happily married, and the point of it might be love saves us all. Keep working on it through a bitter divorce, and it won't be the same novel. Part of this is unavoidable. We are different people today than we will be tomorrow. If you work long enough, the piece can become impossible to finish, something that never will be. When the writer and professional celebrity Truman Capote died, all anyone found of his much-touted last novel was a handful of pages. When noted novelist Ralph Ellison died at eighty, his long-awaited second novel, the follow-up to his classic *The Invisible Man*, was still uncompleted after four decades.

At some point writers have to move on. Leave whatever doubts you still have about a single word or a whole book to the critics and scholars. Start something new.

EXERCISES

1. Use the Macro and Micro Revision Checklists on a piece of fiction you have written. Make notes of what you think works or doesn't work in your piece. Put question marks next to things you are not sure about.

2. Show the piece to a friend, fellow writer, or group of writers. Make careful notes about what they say. Compare them to the notes you made after using the checklists. Make a combined chore list of things that need to be fixed. Concentrate on the larger structural questions, the macro concerns. Don't worry too much yet about how you will fix them.

3. Now go for a long walk or just live your life for a few days or weeks, but keep thinking about your piece. When you feel restless with ideas, return to your desk or computer and begin revising.

4. After you have finished revising, let the piece sit for a while, then

read it beginning to end, preferably aloud. If you have any doubts, go through exercises one, two, and three again.

5. When you are as sure as you can be that you are finished revising, use the Micro Checklist one last time, and always be sure to proofread your final copy carefully. Then start something new.

FORMS AND STRUCTURES

CHAPTER TEN

NOVEL VS. SHORT STORY

S o far I've been talking as if any idea can be turned into either a short story or a novel with equal success. But at some point, every writer has to answer the question, Which form of fiction is best for what I have to say? In the next chapter, we'll discuss less traditional fictional forms, such as the short short story, the novella, and the novel-in-stories, but here let's concentrate on the two most common choices, the novel and the short story. Before you choose let me give you a brief history of each.

THINK BIG

Why are there traditional lengths for fiction at all? It is not as if words naturally travel in certain size groups like herds of buffalo, pods of whales, and life pairs of swans. The answer lies in the history of the printed word. A fiction-writing pilgrimage would have to start in Mainz, Germany, where Gutenberg set up his first press in the 1450s. Modern fiction is a printed medium above all else, and before the availability of printing and the commercial market for books and periodicals that resulted, fiction could not exist in any of the forms we've come to know.

By the nineteenth century, the most popular, mass-produced fictional form was the novel. It was what the people read, sometimes secretly, and for many years was looked down upon as vastly inferior to poetry, which is what the learned folks favored. From the beginning the novel was a commercial form, one of the few ways for authors to earn a living from the sale of their work. Only later did it gain respectability. The form's popular heritage is important to keep in mind because writing a novel is not an academic or narcissistic exercise. Even today people voluntarily buy and read novels more than any other form of fiction.

A novel was and still is any single piece of fiction long enough to merit being printed, bound, and sold by itself, not as a part of a newspaper or magazine, but as something readers would find of sufficient length to purchase alone. Looked at in this light, all the other aspects of this form of fiction (its chapters, subplots, and minor characters) are merely devices that have been developed by writers to structure and fill the necessary number of pages. If a novel needs to be a certain length to be publishable, then writers quickly learn to make good use of the space. Even in fiction, form follows function.

The preferred length of the novel has varied with time and fashion and is still in flux. On a recent trip to a bookstore, I found newly released ones ranging from 175 to 1,250 pages. The trend in literary publishing recently has been to thinner and smaller volumes with publishers citing both the shortened attention span of contemporary readers and the cost of paper, but this is not universal. The craze for brevity has not affected the books of popular authors such as John Irving, Tom Clancy, or Anne Rice. At the moment you would be safe in saying that anything over 200 manuscript pages might be long enough to stand alone and anything under 1,000 pages stands some chance of being published. The average contemporary novel probably runs 300 to 450 manuscript pages.

SHORT STORIES

The short story is a more recent arrival on the commercial literary scene than the novel. Its history is interwoven with the history of the periodical, Sherlock Holmes was introduced to the world by Arthur Conan Doyle in short stories running in the pages of *Strand* magazine in England. O. Henry published his very short stories in turn-of-the-century American newspapers and popular magazines such as *McClure's* and *Outlook*. So if a novel is any work of fiction long enough to be bound and sold alone, then a short story is any work short enough to be published whole in a periodical.

The short story flourished in this way, appearing in periodicals for more than a century. F. Scott Fitzgerald and William Faulkner both wrote magazine stories to finance their less lucrative careers as novelists. More recently the short story has become the staple of creative writing courses, which are now commonplace in American schools and on college campuses. This has led to a much talked about renaissance of the short story. More stories are being written today than ever before, but the majority of these do not appear in the few commercial magazines left that still carry fiction. Instead, they are first published in one of the many wonderful literary magazines where payment is more often in glory than in cash.

These magazines have more room to run fiction than the newspapers of O. Henry's day, but as any editor can tell you, paper and ink aren't free, so the longer a story is, the stronger it had better be. Very long short stories have some structural and plot pecularities more typical of the novel. I'll take them up when I discuss the novella in the next chapter. A quick survey of the yearly anthologies like *Best American Short Stories* turns up selections that originally ran ten to fifty pages in manuscript, with the average story coming in somewhere between fifteen and twenty-five typed double-spaced pages.

When I first started, I wrote stories. I did this because writing workshops usually emphasize short fiction. Even as rigorous and excellent a teacher as Janet Burroway would probably have felt foolish asking us to write a novel by the next week or even by the end of the semester. When I was writing stories, I was vaguely aware of a desire to write a novel some day. I remember thinking that perhaps I would start a short story that just wouldn't end. As I worked on it, it would be at first a long story, then a novella, and finally, *ta-dah*, a novel. A workable theory, but that isn't what happened to me.

Other writers who were my friends all seemed to be starting novels. I was jealous. I felt like the last kid on the block to get the training wheels off my bike. One day after having a talk with a friend who was struggling with the first draft of a novel, I was walking down the stairs from her fourth-floor apartment in a large, drafty old building. I thought to myself, *Damn it. I want to get an idea big enough for a novel.* Before I reached the ground floor, I had one. A woman's husband dies suddenly. Just as suddenly the woman decides to have him cremated and take his ashes with her to Paris. There she would meet another man, not an American. The story would end with a birth of their child.

It wasn't until I was well along with my plotting and planning that I realized what I had really done was take the characters from my story "Underground Women" and set them loose in Paris in 1929. But the differences between the story "Underground Women" and the novel *The Museum of Happiness*, both in their conception and their execution, are really more interesting and instructive than their similarities. They are good examples of the inherent differences in structure of the two forms.

A PERFECT SINGULARITY

Edgar Allan Poe, in his famous 1842 review of Nathaniel Hawthorne's *Tales*, put forward what has come to be the standard critical definition of the short story. He believed that

> the short story is not only not a chapter of a novel, or an incident or an episode extracted from a longer tale, but at its best it impresses the reader with the belief that it would be spoiled if it were made larger or if it were incorporated into a larger work.

By then the short story had been around long enough to establish its essential brevity, and so Poe felt the need to evolve a theory of what a short story needed to be beyond simply short. He thought a short story should have "a certain unique or single effect" and that everything the short story writer did should be calculated to produce it.

> If his very initial sentence tend not to the outbringing of this effect, then he has failed in his first step. In the whole composition there should be no word written, of which the tendency, direct or indirect, is not to the pre-established design. And by such means, with such care and skill, a picture is at length painted which leaves the mind of him who contemplates it with a kindred art, a sense of full satisfaction. The idea of the tale has been presented unblemished, because undisturbed; and this is an end unattainable by the novel.

He wrote that "undue brevity" was to be avoided, but "undue length" even more so. Clayton Hamilton's *A Manual of the Art of Fiction*, a writer's guide published in 1918, paraphrases Poe neatly, stating "the aim of a short story is to produce a single narrative effect with the greatest economy."

How do you know if an idea you have is suited to such an approach? As I mentioned earlier, my short story "Underground Women" was inspired by my seeing a woman on the floor of a Paris laundromat. I wanted to write a story that would make readers feel the way I did when I saw her. In Poe's words it would create "a certain unique or single effect." So I constructed a plot that explained who the dead woman was and established why her life and death mattered. I invented incidents to aid me in establishing my preconceived effect, and then I strove to make sure there was in "the whole composition . . . no word written, of which the tendency, direct or indirect, is not to the pre-established design." In other words if the plot of the story were laid out on a conflict pyramid, all elements of the structure would lead inevitably and directly to the resolution of the internal and external conflicts, to the desired single effect of the story. In the universe of the short story, there is no room to wander or digress.

This single-mindedness in the name of effect is evident in many of the structural elements that make up "Underground Women." It takes place over just a few days and has a single narrator so that time and voice unify the piece. The action revolves around one central incident and takes place in a limited number of locations so that the minimum number of words are needed to set scenes or describe actions. There are a limited number of characters (two major and perhaps four minor ones, two of those dead), something that is certainly true of a typical short story. The conflict is resolved in the last sentence with a crisis action reduced to one small, telling gesture.

In this case the short story ends when Madame Desnos, who has abandoned her hotel to her deadbeat husband, and the narrator stop on a bridge over the Seine near Notre Dame. Their suitcases are at their feet. Madame Desnos has locked the doors of all the rooms in the hotel and taken the keys with her. As they stand on the bridge, the narrator says,

> "Perhaps there are places where it is better for a woman to live."
> Madame Desnos holds one of the brass keys between her long fine fingers and lets it drop into the Seine. "Perhaps,"

she says, and I watch as one by one they fall, golden beads
on a rosary, raising a tiny glinting splash apiece.

This ending is also typical of the contemporary short story in that
it leaves the central characters, especially the narrator, poised on the
edge of change. We do not really know where either the narrator or
Madame Desnos are headed, let alone where they will end up, but we
do know it is forward into a future changed by their meeting. If this
were a novel, we probably wouldn't be content to leave the two main
characters homeless on a bridge. We would need to have a clearer
and more definite idea of their future before the novel ended, but for
a short story, the suggestion of change is usually enough.

To assess whether your idea fits the short form, consider that the
classic short story often

1. covers a limited amount of time
2. involves a limited number of characters
3. occurs in just one or two places
4. has a single narrator or point-of-view character
5. has an external conflict easily and effectively closed with a symbolic object or small gesture
6. leaves your characters on the brink of finally realizing or failing
   to realize the solutions to their internal conflicts

If only some of these are true you still might have a good idea for
a short story. You can achieve Poe's single effect by strong emphasis
on one or more items in this list. Many of the stories we've discussed
earlier in the book work that way. If we go back over the list point by
point, this becomes clear.

A short story covers a limited amount of time. Raymond
Carver's "Are These Actual Miles?" tells the story of Toni and Leo's
entire marriage, but it does this by concentrating exclusively on the
single night when they must sell their car. If you have an idea that
seems too big to be a short story, you can trim it down to a manageable
size by focusing on one crucial night, day, or hour.

A short story involves a limited number of characters.
Ernest Hemingway's "Hills Like White Elephants," with its conversation between a nameless man and woman in an almost depopulated
spot, is a perfect example of this. Other examples are Joy Williams'
"Train" and T. Coraghessan Boyle's "Greasy Lake." If you have an

idea that seems to cover too much space or time, remember you can use character as the unifying element

A short story occurs in just one or two places. In my story "Underground Women," most of the action takes place in Madame Desnos' hotel. The story covers just a few days, but the same principle holds true even if a great deal of time passes. Willa Cather's "Neighbour Rosicky," with its multiple point-of-view characters, is unified by place as well as by everyone's shared concern for the title character. If you have a story that involves many characters or much time, consider using a single setting for unity of effect.

A short story has a single narrator or point-of-view character. As we discussed in the chapters on point of view, short stories commonly have a single narrator or point-of-view character. Just how perfectly this can unify a story is shown in Tillie Olsen's "I Stand Here Ironing," in which the story of a daughter's entire childhood is held together by the mother's narrative voice. If you want to move through a great deal of time or space and still have a unified story, using a strong point-of-view character or narrator can do the trick.

A short story has an external conflict easily and effectively closed with a symbolic object or small gesture. This is true of most of the short stories we have covered and many others. Look at "A Small, Good Thing," by Raymond Carver, and "I Look Out for Ed Wolfe," by Stanley Elkin, just to name two. If you can't think of a way to close your story quite so simply because the idea seems too large or the character complications need a larger resolution, then you may have a novel on your hands.

A short story leaves your characters on the brink of finally realizing or failing to realize the solutions to their internal conflicts. This is one of those acid tests. If you can stand to leave your characters on the brink of change, then you probably have a short story idea. If you are so involved in your characters' lives that many pages are needed for falling action and resolution, you may have an idea more suited to a novel than a story.

NOVEL TECHNIQUES

The Museum of Happiness, unlike "Underground Women," grew out of character, out of my wanting to know what would happen to this young widow I was so determined to send to Paris. In this way *The*

Museum of Happiness is a typical novel, a form that, even more than the short story, is in love with character. A novel is long enough for us to really come to love or hate or pity or fear the characters in it. This is one of the form's great strengths and one of the reasons why most readers prefer it. The list of favorite novels that I asked you to make at the end of chapter one is really an address book in disguise, the titles of the books being the homes of the characters you love. A short story may let us peek at characters' lives, but novels let us live with them. By its nature a novel has to be long enough for readers to see how characters grow and change or, as Gertrude Stein supposedly remarked, to see how people never change.

When I started writing *The Museum of Happiness*, I felt like I was learning to write all over again. For every useful trick I had learned, there were now three I had to unlearn. I exaggerate, but there are essential differences between short stories and novels, most of them simple by-products of length. This becomes clear if we go back over the list of short-story characteristics we used above, this time stated in the negative to show how the same elements would work in a novel, rather than a short story.

A novel need not cover just a limited amount of time. The greater length of the novel demands a different treatment of time. More pages means you will either cover more time than you would in a short story or cover a short amount of time in much greater detail. Gabriel García Márquez's *One Hundred Years of Solitude* covers a century and many generations of the Buendia family and so is a classic example of the "more time" approach. Nicholson Baker's *The Mezzanine*, which covers only a lunch hour, and *One Day in the Life of Ivan Denisovich*, by Aleksandr Solzhenitsyn, which covers a single waking day, would be classic examples of the greater detail approach. A more typical example from contemporary fiction is Jane Hamilton's *A Map of the World*, which covers several crucial months in the life of the husband and wife who are the novel's main characters.

When I first began inventing the plot for *The Museum of Happiness*, I thought that to be a novel, it should, like *One Hundred Years of Solitude*, tell the story of multiple generations. I set the opening of the novel in 1929 to give myself room to run through several sets of lives without the story stretching so far into the future it became science fiction. Later I realized that my novel, like *A Map of the World*, would cover less than a year. By then my story was already too deeply entwined in the events of 1929 to move it. If I had been thinking more clearly, I would have realized a plot does not have to cover one hundred years to be more suitable for a novel than a story. Like me you may find your original idea of how much time your novel will cover to be wrong. In my experience, in the novel you often never quite know what you are up to until you finish a first draft. Relax and give your idea a try, whether it covers a day or a decade.

A novel need not have just a limited number of characters. In the novel more space means more emphasis on character. It will either involve many characters or a few characters treated in great depth. Charles Dickens' *Bleak House* is the extreme example of the former, with its wealth of both point-of-view and non-point-of-view characters. F. Scott Fitzgerald's *The Great Gatsby*, on the other hand, is typical of a novel that explores a limited set of characters in great depth.

When I was writing the first draft of *The Museum of Happiness*, I was so delighted by all the space the novel form provided for characters that I went a bit overboard. Even the most inconsequential character could step into the story delivering a telegram, and I would try to give him a larger part. In revising I had to execute a number of these poor people in the name of tightening the plot. By giving myself that freedom in the first drafts, I invented some wonderful characters who did stay in the novel all the way to the end. If you are unsure if your novel should concentrate on a few or a wealth of characters, I urge you to think big and dare to be Dickensian in your early drafts. You can always thin the crowd when you revise.

A novel need not occur in just one or two places. In a novel you have the freedom to either change settings many times or to develop one place in great detail. Kerouac's *On The Road* does the first, South African writer J.M. Coetzee's *Waiting for the Barbarians*, the second. Most novels fall somewhere in the middle. The primary setting of *The Museum of Happiness* is Paris, but parts are also set in Florida, Alsace, Germany, and in the French town of Le Puy. If you have a place you want readers to spend hundreds of pages getting to know, don't be afraid to stay put, but if your story needs to move, a novel is certainly long enough to handle several shifts of locale. Put your characters in the moving van and go.

A novel need not have just a single narrator or point-of-view character. A novel can have a number of narrators or point-of-view characters. I've already mentioned William Faulkner's *As I Lay Dying* as a tour de force of multiple narrative voices. Gabriel García Márquez's *One Hundred Years of Solitude* is similarly successful in using third-person point of view. Most novels settle for one or two points of view. When I was writing the first draft of *The Museum of Happiness*, I had been so conditioned to avoid multiple points of view in my short stories that I stuck to Ginny's point of view. It slowly dawned on me—much too slowly!—that I couldn't tell the story without adding Roland's point of view. After that breakthrough, I felt liberated enough to add the odd chapter or section told from a minor character's point of view. Every extra point of view you add to your book means having to deal with another pair of conflict pyramids, but in a longer work you have time to deal with such complications. Don't be afraid to try a multiple point of view in your novel. If it doesn't work, you can always change your mind when you revise.

A novel need not have an external conflict easily and effectively closed with a symbolic object or small gesture. As we discussed in the chapter on endings, novels often need a larger final crisis action than do stories. Also remember that novels usually have more falling action and resolution and that the crisis action is more likely to be in the next-to-last chapter than the next-to-last sentence. When I first started to think about how to end my novel, I looked at the ones on my bookshelf. I was shocked by how far the last events I remembered in the novels (Emma Bovary's death, Holden Caulfield's collapse) were from the actual last pages. I remembered the crisis actions, but looking back over the books, I could see how crucial were the subsequent pages spent on falling action and resolution. Review some of the novels you know well. You, too, may be surprised.

A novel need not leave your characters on the brink of finally realizing or failing to realize the solutions to their internal conflicts. Everything I have said about where the crisis action is in a novel is also true of the internal crisis. The most important point to remember about internal conflict in novels, as opposed to short stories, is that whether the characters get or don't get what they want, the end is usually more permanent. They don't just get what they want temporarily, and they don't just get a promise of satisfaction someday. Happiness or unhappiness, success or failure, may be transitory even in novels, but Emma Bovary isn't coming back from the dead. The finality of her fate is typical of novel endings.

BUILDING CHAPTERS

It seems too obvious to mention, but novels are usually divided into chapters. Stories are not. This turns out to be one of the most essential differences in their structures. When I began writing my first novel, even though I had read novels all my life, I realized I really didn't know what a chapter did or even how long one should be. Again I pulled books off my shelf. I sat counting pages and found chapters ranging in length from four pages to forty. Even within the same book, the length of the chapters often varied significantly. I saw that a chapter could be almost any length.

Then I read chapters from various novels and developed a theory that the chapter was rather like the paragraph. It was a device designed to break prose in a book into related and manageable chunks in the same way the paragraph structures words and ideas on a page. I reasoned that like a short story, a chapter in a novel can usually be read in a single uninterrupted sitting, so it should also have a certain single effect.

As a reader I knew I almost never stopped reading in the middle of a novel chapter unless I was interrupted. I read on to the end of the chapter even if that meant staying up late or putting off a necessary task. I also knew that a chapter's ending in a well-written book was never so satisfying that I put down the book and called it quits before I got to the very end. This last point made me suspect that a chapter was not a variety of short story and didn't have a complete conflict pyramid. But when it came to plotting what would happen in each chapter in my novel or even planning how many chapters there would be, I was at a bit of a loss.

Theory only gets you so far in writing. Then you have to roll up your sleeves and find out by doing. I wrote first one chapter and then another. I was a hundred pages into the first draft when I realized I was not only opening most of my chapters with Ginny waking up, I was also closing them with her going to bed. Each chapter began with *the alarm clock rang* and lasted until *she set the alarm and turned out the light*. I was covering too much daily boring detail at the start of each chapter (she got dressed, had breakfast, and so on), and each chapter was ending too completely, with enough conflict resolved for her to get yet another good night's sleep. If Ginny set out after breakfast to find a cemetery in Paris for her dead husband's ashes, by night she would have found it. I could imagine my readers yawning by the hundreds and saying, "My, wasn't that satisfying," and closing their books at the end of the chapter, never to open them again.

I went back and cut all those comfortable breakfasts, and I re-arranged the chapter breaks. I discovered a basic fact of writing novel chapters: Each one needs a hook, an unresolved conflict to pull readers into the next chapter. There are indeed separate conflict pyramids within the larger structure of the novel (for different char-acters, for subplots), but it is better not to have their resolutions coincide with the end of a chapter. Resolve one conflict in the middle of a chapter, then introduce another. Or have a character think the conflict is resolved in the middle of the chapter only to find at the end that nothing has changed or that the situation has gotten even worse. Or resolve one but make it clear by the conclusion of the chapter that a problem from an earlier chapter is still fatefully pending.

My earliest version of the novel opens with a long dreamy sequence before Ginny learns her husband has died (more alarm clock), but in the final version I decided to open in midaction, to jump Into the Pot, Already Boiling, with this first sentence, which I quoted previously in the chapter on openings.

> In the morgue, Ginny Gillespie took a step forward and laid a finger on her husband Paul's cheek, touched a corner of his mouth where death had caught him blank-faced, too busy to smile or frown.

The immediate external conflict introduced in the first chapter is, What will Ginny do with Paul's body? Where will she bury him, and where will she live her life as a widow? The internal conflict is the larger question of what she is going to do with her life. The end of the chapter solves the immediate external conflict but leaves the resolution to her internal conflict open—so open, I hope, that no reader will be able to stop reading. In it Ginny announces to the funeral director her intention to have Paul cremated, not the usual procedure in Florida in 1929. She is handed a form to fill out to justify her decision.

> Ginny paused, the point of the fat, black pen Mr. McCue handed her poised above the paper, then she wrote:
> *I am going to Paris.*
> It just fit.

What reader wouldn't want to go to Paris, I reasoned, and left it at that.

Early drafts of the second chapter followed Ginny as she got ready to leave Florida and as she sailed on the *Ile de France* on her way to Paris. These incidents are also no longer in the finished novel. Instead chapter two introduces Roland two decades in the past and five thousand miles away. I did this so readers would know early on that there would be two major point-of-view characters. In doing so I discovered the happy by-product that whenever you weave two narratives, tension is created. It acts as a strong hook for readers who wonder when and how these two stories will intersect and these two completely different people meet. The chapter opens with Roland's birth.

> When Lena Keppi had been in labor thirteen hours, she opened her eyes and saw her mother-in-law Odile lift her baby from her. She saw Odile's webbed hand touched with her blood, then she saw her son's hand was webbed too. In that tiny hand, Lena saw her future. There had always been Keppis in Alsace, before Caesar, before anything. But she, fresh from Germany, full of plans for owning—a house, a vineyard, anything, everything—would not get to stay. It was July 27, 1906.

And it ends with Roland in a boy's boarding school on the French-German border worried about his father who has joined the Kaiser's army.

> Four days after his father's letter, Roland took his place in Herr Epfig's room to find he was facing not a map of ancient Gaul, but one of Germany, Belgium, France. Red arrows poured down from Aachen into Belgium. "The army has moved into Belgium to defend Belgium from France," Herr

Epfig said. It was August 1, 1914.

War.

Max, Roland sent the thought up like a reconnaissance bal-
loon. Where was his father?

If this chapter closed with Roland and his father safe, the war over, it
wouldn't have the hook this ending provides.

When I say novel chapters need hooks to keep readers interested,
remember that these can be ongoing external or internal conflicts or,
best of all, a clever combination of the two. If you have any doubts
about how to build ongoing conflicts into your novel chapters, look at
a good mystery novel, a form that lives or dies on plot. Mysteries tend
to emphasize the external conflict (the search for the murderer) over
the internal (the search for meaning in life), but no published mystery
writer would let a chapter end without something urging readers to
read on, preferably late into the night.

EXERCISES

1. Review the list of Potential Story Ideas you made after reading
chapter one. Which seem better for a short story? Which better for a
novel? Choose one idea and outline a plot using conflict pyramids or
scene-by-scene or chapter-by-chapter notes to make it into first a short
story, then a novel.

2. Choose an idea from the same list (or from your experience)
that seems too large for a short story (the story of someone's whole
life, of a country or a people) and come up with some small part of it
that can stand for the larger whole, one day in someone's life, one
town in all of Germany. Plot this as a short story.

3. Choose an idea from the list (or from your experience) that
seems too small for a novel (getting a haircut, taking a class field trip),
and list enough details about the real or imagined experience to fill a
novel. Make up at least two major characters and outline the external
and internal conflicts they have that revolve around this simple incident. Write a paragraph from first one character's point of view, then
from the other's.

4. Read the first and last paragraph of each chapter of a novel you
know well. Write down what conflicts you think are resolved at the
conclusion of each chapter, which new ones introduced or continued.

Ask yourself at the conclusion of each chapter, Why do I want to keep reading?

5. Rewrite all or part of one of your short stories as if it were a chapter of a novel. Make sure not to resolve the conflict at the end.

6. Choose a published novel and try rearranging it into longer chapters. Where would the new divisions be? How does that change the way the book reads? Now try shorter chapters. Does this make the novel read faster, or does it seem choppy?

CHAPTER ELEVEN

SHORT SHORTS, NOVELLAS, NOVELS-IN-STORIES

S o far we have been discussing fiction as if it only came in two
sizes, large (novels) and small (short stories), but there are other
possibilities for building fiction, each with its own particular structure.
In this chapter I'll talk about three alternative forms: the short short
story, the novella, and the novel-in-stories. I discussed short stories
and novels first because the three alternative forms are defined in
opposition to short stories and novels as well as by how they resemble
them.

Why the urge to experiment with length and form? Why not be
content to write either short stories or novels? Some writers are born
contrary. The same impulse that led humans to record their imagina-
tive views of life in the first place led them to invent rules for the forms
and then, just as instinctively, want to break them. We'll discuss the
broader implications of this instinct for experimentation in the last
chapter of this book, but the same basic artistic restlessness is at work
here.

SHORT SHORTS

In the nineteenth century a short story was more likely to run 1,500
words than the 5,000 words contemporary short stories average. This
growth was due in part to the increasing sophistication of the short
story audience, which grew tired of the trick endings favored by
writers like O. Henry. (For example, in "The Gift of the Magi," a girl
sells her hair to buy her beloved a watch chain only to learn he sold

his watch to buy her a hair comb.) Writers began to emphasize internal conflict over external, to stress believable character development over plot twists. As we know from our discussions on character, bringing people to life on the page requires more space than 1,500 words.

But a few decades ago, some writers began working back the other way. In the 1970s an issue of *The New Yorker* hardly seemed complete without one of the odd tales by the short-short-story master Donald Barthelme. He was part of a group of writers who were interested in creating *metafiction*, fiction that called attention to the artificiality of traditional narrative structure. Because of this approach, his work is often experimental in ways other than length, but it is quite strikingly succinct, with most stories running no more than a few typeset pages. His short short stories were eventually collected in two wonderful volumes, *Sixty Stories* and *Forty Stories*. Though brief, his stories did not return to the use of trick or surprise endings. Instead, they had their own odd, character-based plots built on internal and external conflicts, the same structure we've seen in the short stories we've discussed.

Typical is Barthelme's story "At the End of the Mechanical Age," which features in its opening paragraph a first encounter that is a parody of all fictional romance, but succeeds in being heartfelt in its own offbeat way.

> I went to the grocery store to buy some soap. I stood for a long time before the soaps in their attractive boxes, RUB and FAB and TUB and suchlike, I couldn't decide so I closed my eyes and reached out blindly and when I opened my eyes I found her hand in mine.
>
> Her name was Mrs. Davis, she said, and TUB was best for important cleaning experiences, in her opinion.

Then in seven pages, the narrator and Mrs. Davis exchange their philosophies of life, get married at a wedding God himself attends, and decide marriage is not really possible at the end of the mechanical age. In other words, through extreme use of Poe's principal of single effect, Barthelme tells the entire story of the narrator and Mrs. Davis' life together with great economy. The narrator and Mrs. Davis, having fallen in love with other people, send their son, A.F. of L. Davis, "to that part of Russia where people live to be one hundred and ten years old." The story ends as the narrator and Mrs. Davis shake hands and part, while standby generators ensure "the flow of grace to all of God's creatures at the end of the mechanical age." This short short story uses a gesture (shaking hands) to close the external conflict, a comes-to-realize ending (they are not meant for each other) for its internal conflict. Structurally it behaves just like its longer cousins.

If we examine Barthelme's opening, we can see the two ways the great economy of narrative is achieved. In the first fifty-four words, the narrator meets his future wife. If an ordinary short story has to establish the external and internal conflicts quickly, then a short short story has to explode out of the gate. The first rule for making a story into a successful short short is to start fast and to keep running through the normal ups and downs of the plot with equal rapidity.

The second secret is tight control of language. Short shorts do not have room for extra adjectives, for long passages of description. This does not mean they are devoid of detail—quite the contrary. It means that each detail has to do the work of legions. Barthelme has carefully chosen his *RUB* and *TUB* and they stand in place of a longer description of the store. Indeed they stand for the entire modern world at the sad end of the mechanical age. When writing a short short, you need to choose details as carefully as you'd pack for a trip where your luggage is limited to one small carry-on bag.

Not every short short is humorous nor are all the characters and situations so unusual. What every writer gains from the form is the ability to stick to the essentials, to use only the one or two best of everything (lines of dialogue, images, scenes) that are the diamond-hard heart of a story without having to do the usual work of writing pages of background and development. Poets interested in telling stories and already accustomed to economy of form are often drawn to the short short story. I find it both a challenge and a treat. When I am in the middle of a novel, a project that can take years, I find writing a short short story provides the perfect break.

THE SMALLEST OF THE SMALL

In recent years the short short story has experienced a renaissance similar to the one enjoyed by the more traditional short story. Literary magazines began to feature short shorts, and a few anthologies of short short fiction appeared, sold well, and were joined by others. Most of these stories run from three to five typed pages. Poe may have been right when he wrote that in short stories undue brevity was to be avoided, but contemporary short-short-story writers seem to love to push the envelope, to ask the question, How short is too short?

The shortest run a single typed page, usually under 300 words. These stories are particularly instructive because they allow us fiction writers to do what we seldom can: see and study a whole story on one page. In this brief form, every word counts. After you write a one-page story, you will find it hard to let a weak and unnecessary adjective or even a stray conjunction like *but* or *and* wander into your fiction again. These one pagers are useful to examine because they show the two ways to get the compression needed in short short stories: They either are summary based, using detail to sketch a story that takes place over a larger stretch of time, or they are based on single scenes that imply a larger narrative.

Barthelme's "At the End of the Mechanical Age" is summary based. So is this one-page story, "Worry," by poet and fiction writer Ron Wallace. Both prove that even whole lives are not too big a subject for this most concise of fictional forms.

WORRY

She worried about people; he worried about things. And between them, that about covered it.

"What would you think of our daughter sleeping around?" she said.

"The porch steps are rotting," he replied. "Someone's going to fall through."

They were lying in bed together, talking. They had been lying in bed together talking these twenty-five years. First about whether to have children, he wanted to (although the roof was going fast); she didn't (Down's Syndrome, leukemia, microcephalia, mumps). Then, after their daughter was born, a healthy seven pounds eleven ounces ("She's not eating enough"; "The furnace is failing"), they talked about family matters, mostly ("Her friends are hoodlums, her room is a disaster"; "There's something about the brakes, the water heater's rusting out.")

Worry grew between them like a son, with his own small insistencies and then more pressing demands. They stroked and coddled him; they set a place for him at the table; they sent him to kindergarten, private school, and college. Because he failed at nearly everything and always returned home, they loved him. After all, he was their son.

"I've been reading her diary. She does drugs. She sleeps around."

"I just don't think I can fix them myself. Where will we find a carpenter?"

Their daughter married her high school sweetheart, had a family, and started a health food store in a distant town. Although she recalled her childhood as fondly as anyone— how good her parents had been and how they worried for her, how old and infirm they must be growing, their house going to ruin—she rarely called or visited. She had worries of her own.

By *summary based* I do not mean that a story has no detail, merely that each detail stands as an example for many similar occurrences. Wallace's story "Worry" begins with a thesis, what in chapter two I called an Opening Statement to the Jury: "She worried about people; he worried about things. And between them, that about covered it." Then it provides typical lines of dialogue, both directly and in summary form, to prove the opening thesis true. In its 273 words, the story tells the history of an entire marriage and of three lives. This brief form is perfect for thesis- or idea-based fiction (worry does no good, love doesn't last, and so on). It gives you a chance to make your point and get out, a point that might become tedious in a longer work of fiction.

While "Worry" is summary based, covering a large stretch of time, "Stone Belly Girl," by Jamie Granger, uses the opposite strategy. It is scene based, covering a very limited time and merely implying the larger future of the characters.

STONE BELLY GIRL

That year when the St. Kitts carnival came around, the stone belly girl had a cold. Three months before, she'd begun to bleed down there, and her aunt had explained to her all that that meant. And even though she had told her father no, not this year, she held his big calloused hand—his other grasped the hammer—as they mounted the wooden steps to the stage. Before the grandstand, the children, policemen, and steel drum band, the mothers, masqueraders, and the soft drink and Sno Cone stands, she waited for the crowd to subside, like the sea sometimes did before it rained.

Then the stone belly girl got down on her back, sniffled, and lifted her thin cotton dress toward her narrow chest. This dress was so unlike the gowns the girls in the Miss St. Kitts Pageant wore. But she'd worn it every year since the first, when her father, loud and drunk, had pushed her into the mud behind the grandstand and busted a small flat rock on her stomach with a nailhammer. Now her father came toward her with the big rounded stone, smooth as a calabash in his hands, and lowered it gently down, sea salt glistening on its black skin, onto her brown belly. The stone belly girl wanted to blow her nose, but instead relaxed under the weight, as she had learned to do, and watched the polished hammerhead go up and come down. Once and then once more before the stone broke like an egg, the two halves rolling off her, and she stood up and coughed.

Since Granger has less time to cover, he has more room for detailed description: "Before the grandstand, the children, policemen, and steel drum band, the mothers, masqueraders, and the soft drink and Sno Cone stands, she waited for the crowd to subside." He has more room for internal character development as well, going into the central character's head: "The stone belly girl wanted to blow her nose, but instead relaxed under the weight, as she had learned to do, and watched the polished hammerhead go up and come down." Even so, the 266 words he uses do not allow him the time or space to delve too deeply.

The challenge of the scene-based short short story is to make a relatively brief moment seem complete, not just a page from a larger work. Granger does this by creating an immediate and clear external conflict. Worried that the girl will be injured, we read on to see what will happen and are relieved when the stone splits in two. He also creates an internal conflict; the girl does not want to perform this trick. She isn't a girl any longer, but a woman. She feels instinctively that her future is not with her father at the fair. It is no accident that the first rock her father broke on her is described as small and flat while this one is as round and smooth as a pregnant belly. But when the rock breaks in two like an egg, the two halves rolling off her, and she stands and coughs, we are left to wonder if she has any future besides as a stone belly girl.

If you have a scene that you have always wanted to use in a story but that always seemed too vivid or self-contained, it may be perfect for a scene-based short short story. As in "Stone Belly Girl," the careful choice of detail is all-important in creating this kind of miniature world. Remember too that whatever comes last (action, gesture, thought, or dialogue) must provide the same sense of closure it would in a longer story.

Just to prove I wouldn't suggest you try something I wouldn't, here is the only one-page short short story I've ever managed to write, weighing in at 276 words. It, too, is an example of a scene-based story, though the ending is more clearly predictive of the characters' futures than Granger's.

CARPATHIA

It happened on my parents' honeymoon. The fourth morning out from New York, Mother woke to find the *Carpathia* still, engines silent. She woke Father; they rushed to the deck in their nightgowns. The first thing they saw was the white of an ocean filled with ice, then they saw white boats, in groups of two or three, pulling slowly toward the *Carpathia*. My father read the name written in red across their bows— *Titanic*. The sun was shining. Here and there a deck chair floated on the calm sea. There was nothing else.

The survivors came on board in small groups. Women and

children. Two sailors for each boat. The women of the *Carpathia* went to the women of the *Titanic*, wrapping them in their long warm furs. My mother left my father's side to go to them. The women went down on their knees on the deck and prayed, holding each other's children. My father stood looking at the icy water where, if he had been on the other ship, he would be.

When the *Carpathia* dropped off the survivors in New York, my parents too got off and took the train home, not talking much, the honeymoon anything but a success. At the welcome home party, my father got drunk. When someone asked about the *Titanic*, he said, "They should have put the men in the lifeboats. Men can marry again, have new families. What's the use of all those widows and orphans?" My mother, who was standing next to him, turned her face away. She was pregnant, eighteen. She was the one drowning. But there was no one there to rescue her.

So why not try a short short story? Either a one-page short short like these examples or a three- to five-page short short. If you start out only to find your plot barely underway on page five, relax. You haven't wasted your time. You've just written the opening to a regular short story. But if your story is truly a short short, written and plotted so cleverly, so tightly it could be nothing else, then no one will find your story too brief. Instead they will find themselves in agreement with Poe that what you have written is not "an incident or an episode extracted from a longer tale," but a work of art in its own right that "impresses the reader with the belief that it would be spoiled if it were made larger."

THE NOVELLA

When I said in the previous chapter that I used to believe that one day I would start a short story only to find it getting longer and longer until, *surprise*, I had written a novel, I could have been discussing the intermediate and problematic form of the novella. To me the novella's uncertain place in literature is symbolized by the never-ending search for something better to call it. *Novelette* enjoyed a vogue, and now there is a publishing house that promotes a contest for the best *Nivola*.

Like a short short story, a novella is defined most often and easily by what it is not. It is any work of fiction too long to be conveniently published in a periodical as a short story, but not long enough to be published alone as a book. In the current publishing climate, that means a novella is roughly anything over 50 manuscript pages and under 150.

Wherever writers gather one hears the moans of those who have written such an inconveniently sized piece of fiction, but all is not lost. Lately the form has gathered sufficient attention for there to be a number of contests geared specifically to it, such as the annual *Quarterly West* novella competition. It is also becoming increasingly common for authors to publish either collections of novellas or to include one or more in a collection of short stories. Renowned writers Jane Smiley, Ethan Canin, and Charlie Smith have all published well-received books featuring at least one novella.

Beyond the writer's usual perversity, you might ask, Why would anyone want to write something that will be harder to get published than either a novel or a short story? Because the novella is a wonderful form, combining the short story's singleness of effect with the novel's greater room for character and plot development. It is also a natural progression for many writers who find it a step on the way from the short story to the novel. You may find this is true for you, too.

Be forewarned, though, that the novella can be a deceptively easy form. The story writer is inclined to say, "Oh I see, it's just like a very long short story," and proceed to pad a perfectly good story with many extra, unneeded pages. A novelist is apt to say, "Oh, it's just like a cute, baby novel," and compress a larger project down to an indigestible cube of prose. There are crucial ways in which a novella is unlike a story and equally important ways in which it differs from a novel.

Novella vs. Short Story

The first difference between a novella and a short story is how conflict is established in the opening pages. From the beginning a novella establishes either a more complicated conflict or takes more time to establish one. The language is sometimes richer since there is more space for description, but this is not a given. Ethan Canin's "Accountant" opens with a first-person confession, or near confession.

> I am an accountant, that calling of exactitude and scruple, and my crime was small. I have worked diligently, and I do not mind saying that in the conscientious embrace of the ledger I have done well for myself over the years, yet now I must also say that due to a flaw in my character I have allowed one small trespass against my honor. . . . this flaw is so large that it cannot properly be called a flaw but my character itself, and this trespass was devious. I have a wife and three children. My name is Abba Roth.

Notice we are already one long paragraph into the piece and have no idea what the exact nature of the conflict is, the accountant's flaw. This is quite different from the more typical short-story opening of Raymond Carver's "Are These Actual Miles?": "Fact is the car needs to be sold in a hurry, and Leo sends Toni out to do it." If you have an idea for a conflict that may take some space to establish and that you don't want to risk oversimplifying in the name of brevity and concision, then the novella may be the perfect form for you.

There is also extra time and space to develop the conflicts, time for more highs and lows in both the external and internal ones. An episode that could serve as the external crisis action or the crisis of the internal conflict in a short story might well be only one of many such moments in a novella. In Jane Smiley's well-known novella "The Age of Grief," the narrator suspects Dana, his wife and the mother of his three daughters, of having an affair. Dana returns to their summer house hours late.

> Headlights flared across the porch and she drove up with a resolute crunch of gravel. The car door opened. She seemed to leap out and fly up the steps, throw open the door to the dark house, and vanish.

The narrator leaves the house without being seen, hides in the woods, leaving his wife alone to deal with the children. In a short story this could very well serve as the crisis action. The straying wife returns, but the husband flees. In Smiley's novella this action is followed by a long passage of internal reflection. The narrator stands outside his house and his family, looking in and thinking about all they mean to him.

It seemed to me that if I could stay outside forever she would never tell me that she was going to leave me, but that if I joined them inside the light and the warmth, the light and warmth themselves would explode and disappear.

This passage could be the internal crisis of a short story, the comes-to-realize or fails-to-realize at the end leaving the narrator on the edge of change. But in "The Age of Grief," it is only one such episode among many, only one element in the plot. The length of the form allows for a larger slice of life, the hour-by-hour complications of this marriage in crisis. If you have a story to tell that needs to be long enough for readers to see the ups and downs of the plot in greater detail than is possible in a short story, the novella can give you the space that you need.

The most striking and important difference between a short story and a novella is in the ending, in the placement and nature of the resolution. When I was in graduate school, a fellow student was working on a novella. Two down-and-out men, one older, one younger, meet and try to rob a liquor store. The novella ran close to a hundred pages. We read it in several installments in that semester's writing workshop. We followed the older alcoholic as he panhandled, begged for food, slept on the streets and in shelters, and showed the young man how to do likewise. We learned about the older man's ex-wife, now a social worker, and listened along with him to the young man's tales of his childhood psychiatric history. We heard the older man entertain the younger with fishing tales from his life in the old days, to which the younger responded with accounts of his schizophrenic visions. We were there when the younger found the loaded gun that gave him the idea to hold up the liquor store and when the older man agreed, against his better judgment, to go along for fear the younger man would do something fatally stupid. We were hooked.

But when we got to the end of the last installment, we all protested vociferously. The writer ended the piece at the moment the pair stepped into the liquor store. To him the moment before the robbery seemed like the perfect place to stop, the older man opening the door, the perfect crisis action. After all it was already clear the pair was headed into serious trouble. Either they would be shot or arrested or both. Why bother with the last gory details? the writer reasoned.

If he had been writing a short story, he might have been right. Just opening the door meant the older man had given in to the young man's foolish delusions. If he did it while thinking how wonderful it would be to buy tackle with the stolen money and take a bus into the country and have fish for their dinner, the internal crisis would be fails-to-realize. If he opened the door knowing he would never teach his deranged young friend anything, but unable to leave him alone to his fate, it would be comes-to-realize. Either way we would be leaving him on the brink of his fate, poised on the edge of change.

But this was a novella, not a short story, and we had just spent a hundred pages learning all about these two men. It mattered to us whether they were wounded or killed or sent to prison. It mattered what the older man thought as he saw the clerk raise his shotgun, as he was shot or watched his friend get shot, as he was calmly arrested or violently beaten. It mattered who lived and who died. If you are writing a novella, remember to leave room for readers to come to terms with what has happened to your characters, to leave room for falling action and resolution, for an ending that resembles a novel's more than it does a short story's.

Novella vs. Novel

The short story, Poe noted, was not divided into chapters and so there were no places where readers could logically break to leave the fictional world for the real one. Poe believed the most important difference between the short story and the novel was that the story could be read at a single sitting, and thus the events of readers' real lives had no opportunity to dilute or interfere with the author's intended single effect. Similarly novellas rarely have anything resembling chapter breaks, though sometimes one section is separated from another by white space. Though they are sometimes too long to be read conveniently in one sitting, they retain much of the short story's unbroken intensity, its singularity of effect.

That novellas do not usually have chapters may seem a petty point, based purely in the traditions of printing, but the simplest practical reasons for the existence of certain forms tend to take on a greater significance. A novella is much more like a story in having one overarching set of internal and external conflicts leading to a single resolution. It generally doesn't have multiple sets of conflict pyramids, in which one internal or external conflict is resolved only to be replaced by another, the way a novel does. One good reason to write a novella rather than a novel is to take advantage of this continuity of narrative structure. The lack of breaks in "The Age of Grief" mirrors the narrator's own inability to escape from the problems in his marriage. The form makes the readers feel all the more keenly the narrator's broken-hearted and desperate desire to retain both his wife and the life they have built.

If the story you want to tell is too complex for a short story, but would benefit from having some of a short story's intensity of effect, then the novella is the form for you.

A Last Word on Novellas

Look at the novella and the advice I've given you regarding it as existing on a continuum. If you are writing a novella barely fifty pages long, it will necessarily resemble a story structurally more than it does a novel. The opening may be more leisurely, the conflict take a few paragraphs to crystalize, but it still cannot afford to be slow. The middle may involve more scenes, but the complications of the internal and external conflicts will still lead fairly directly to the internal crisis, the external crisis action, and their resolution. The ending will still need to allow time for falling action and resolution, but the crisis action is more likely to take place two paragraphs from the end than ten pages.

If your novella is 150 pages long, it starts to have much more in common structurally with the novel. The opening may take several pages to establish the external conflict, and the internal conflict may be revealed even more slowly. The middle may involve more rise and fall of plot actions, with whole scenes and reflections on the part of the narrator or point-of-view characters leading into other scenes rather than directly to the internal crisis and external crisis action. The ending will need to allow considerable time for falling action and resolution, if still something less than the one to three chapters that would be the normal amount of falling action in a novel.

THE NOVEL-IN-STORIES

The last alternate form, the novel-in-stories, has a history that is the opposite of the short short story or the novella in one respect. I said those forms grew up almost in opposition to their lack of commercial potential. The novel-in-stories is a form that exists partially as a marketing device. You can almost imagine some editor, knowing how reluctant the reading public is to buy short story collections, saying, *Here on my desk is a collection of stories that are all about one family* (or town or central character) *and each story adds something to our knowledge of the family* (or town or central character), *almost the way chapters in a novel do. So, why not say on the jacket that the book is A Novel-in-Stories?* (He immediately rings for the head of the sales department.)

The early 1990s saw a rush of books marketed in this way, but this is not the entire history of the form. A much earlier example is Mary McCarthy's 1942 novel, *The Company She Keeps*, which explores one woman's life in a series of stories told from differing third-, first-, and even second-person points of view. Writers have often found that they had more than one story to tell about a family, a group of people, a city, or a single interesting character. You might have already found that writing one story on a subject only gives you ideas for more. In the past two decades or so, this natural tendency has been reinforced by the growth of graduate writing programs, which usually require their students to complete a book-length work of fiction as their master's thesis. Many writers respond to this challenge by putting together those short stories they feel work best together, and often these stories share a common character, theme, subject, or setting. In other words, the stories are linked in some way. Like the renewed popularity of the short story itself, this idea that short stories can or should be linked has spread beyond the narrow confines of academic writing.

One of the first of these linked collections of stories to gain attention as a new form of novel was Susan Minot's *Monkeys*, published in 1986. This book tells the story of the Vincent family, composed of an alcoholic father, a strong, doting mother, and their seven children. The stories are titled, rather than numbered like chapters, and many were first published separately as short stories. Most could stand alone as complete stories. But taken together these incidents from the family's life form a larger arc, a connect-the-dots conflict pyramid that allows readers to construct an accurate picture of the family over time.

Using this technique a novel-in-stories can achieve a far larger sweep of narrative, cover more time, more characters, more conflicts, more points of view, than any single story. Other excellent examples of the form include Kelly Cherry's *My Life and Dr. Joyce Brothers* and Tom Chiarella's *Foley's Luck*.

Why not just turn the same material into a traditional novel? Well, one practical answer is that the form allows a writer to benefit from both the immediate satisfaction of writing and publishing individual stories and that of eventually completing a larger work. If you commit yourself to a novel, you will spend months or years writing hundreds of pages with no assurance you will complete the project successfully, let alone get it published. If this idea scares you, you are both perfectly sane and a good candidate to try writing a novel-in-stories instead. That way if you find you've run out of steam after three stories instead of the planned ten, at least you will have three perfectly good short stories.

A more high-minded reason to choose the form has to do with what I called the connect-the-dots quality of its larger narrative structure. Because the book is made up of stories, much of the meanwhile-back-at-the-ranch type of transition that connects chapters is absent. You can show an incident from one character's perspective, then shift to another time and place from someone else's point of view and never refer to the first incident again. You can show a crucial scene from your character's childhood (as Chiarella does in *Foley's Luck*) and then jump to twenty years later. Or you can tell a story from an adolescent girl's point of view, then jump back in time to a story narrated by the girl's future mother. The novel-in-stories is essentially an impressionistic form, and it is up to readers to stand back far enough to be able to see that the dots form the portrait of a family or a life.

EXERCISES

1. Write a one-page short short story. We've discussed the basics of the short short story form; now it's time to try one. Make it as close to 300 words as possible. (The title doesn't count, by the way, so one tried-and-true trick is to use a long descriptive title. The first winner of the World's Best Short Short Contest run by Florida State University was a story by Michael Martone titled, "The Mayor of the Sister City Speaks to the Chamber of Commerce in Klamath Falls, Oregon.")

2. Review your list of Potential Story Ideas from chapter one. Are any thesis-based and so would benefit from the condensed treatment of the summary-based short short story? Do any seem as if they are

single memorable scenes and so would make good scene-based short short stories? Using either an idea from your list or a brand new inspiration, write a short short that is three to five pages long. If you need inspiration, look at examples in some of the anthologies now available.

3. Look over your list of Potential Story Ideas again. Do any seem like novella ideas? If so outline a plot that would take your idea beyond the short story into novella territory. To help you do this, find and read at least one novella.

4. Once more, look over your list of Potential Story Ideas. Do any of these ideas share a common character, theme, subject, or setting? Get out any stories you have written. Could any of these be linked? Outline a plan for a series of linked stories. Find and read one novel-in-stories or a collection of connected short stories.

CHAPTER TWELVE

EXPERIMENTAL FICTION

I sometimes think writers experiment with the structure of fiction because we are easily bored. Don't get me wrong. This is a good trait. The first person who ever consciously made up a story, perhaps of a great but imaginary hunt, probably did it to liven up a rainy day when nothing much was going on. If humans did not possess this innate desire to experiment, architecturally we wouldn't have progressed farther than living in lean-tos and rough huts. Fiction writers are people who can never leave well enough alone, and if there is a rule, inevitably some writer is just itching to break it.

At other times I think some writers experiment not so much out of boredom or sheer perversity, but for the same reason we all write, to show other people how we see things and to convince them we are right or that they sometimes see things that way too. Like innovative architects we experiment because we believe the shape of our constructions will improve the lives of the people who dwell in or merely visit them.

In the first case, boredom leads to experimental writing whose main purpose is to break the mold and show the artificiality of the narrative traditions that have built up over time. The second impulse, the desire to present our vision of reality, leads to experimental writing whose main purpose is to adjust the way readers see the whole wide world, not just how they look at fiction. The most successful experimental writing bravely sets out to do both.

Experimental fiction is innovative structurally. Fiction whose subject matter is merely shocking or original is not necessarily experimental. If a short story or novel has more graphic sex or violence in it than any fiction that has come before or if it occurs on a weird planet inhabited by sentient pink vapors but is still traditionally told, it is not experimental fiction. The innovation in structure can be in small details of language or in the larger narrative structure. In this chapter I'll talk about both the large and small, the macro and micro, approaches to experimentation.

EXPERIMENTAL STRUCTURES

You don't have to write a traditional story or novel that begins at the beginning and marches in neat paragraphs to its conclusion just because that's how everybody does it. You can challenge any of the larger elements of structure. The famous twentieth-century architect Le Corbusier called houses "machines for living" and took the steamship and airplane as architectural models. In doing so he questioned deeply held architectural tenets, but for him nothing was too sacred to be cast aside in the name of dwellings that functioned better. Like Frank Lloyd Wright, he was a man with a mission. This doesn't mean either of them was without playfulness and wit. You can experiment just to see how much you can get away with for the pure joy of disobeying the injunctions of your fiction-writing forbears. You can play the talented, but slightly naughty, fair-haired boy.

This is clearly true of a story like "The Glass Mountain," by Donald Barthelme, which is not only experimental in structure, but openly mocks that traditional theory of narrative, the Freytag Pyramid. In it the narrator climbs what is clearly a surreal mountain and an embodiment of classic narrative structure.

1. I was trying to climb the glass mountain.
2. The glass mountain stands at the corner of Thirteenth Street and Eighth Avenue.
3. I had attained the lower slope.
4. People were looking up at me.
5. I was new in the neighborhood.

The narrator overcomes great tribulations, the people below calling him names and the attack of an eagle until he spies at last a glittering palace, and in a moment of pure epiphany a door opens and he sees an "enchanted symbol."

> 97. I approached the symbol . . . but when I touched it, it changed into only a beautiful princess.
> 98. I threw the beautiful princess headfirst down the mountain to my acquaintance.
> 99. Who could be relied upon to deal with her.
> 100. Nor are eagles plausible, not at all, not for a moment.

As he approaches his symbol, it turns from the ideal to the real, from symbol into "only a beautiful princess," reversing what we try to do when we invest ordinary objects (glass slippers) with great meaning. The narrator tosses the princess to the jeering crowd below and dismisses the very possibility of fiction: "Nor are eagles [or glass mountains topped by symbols] plausible, not at all, not for a moment." In this story Barthelme takes the hidden structure of traditional narrative, makes it visible and obviously ridiculous. Along the way he has a whole lot of fun. Let "The Glass Mountain" stand as a challenge and a warning. Any rule or bit of sage advice in this book was born to be broken. I urge you to give it your best. Write a good story that breaks every rule, and I'll buy you your own fourteen-carat-gold symbol. I promise.

You can also break the rules of story structure because you believe you have a story to tell that cannot be told in the conventional way. When I was first in graduate school, I wrote a short story called "A Story Set in Germany" that made Rust Hills, the fiction editor of *Esquire*, who was teaching there that semester, call me the last living metafictionist. This was an exaggeration since all the metafictionists (Donald Barthelme, Robert Coover, John Barth, Gilbert Sorrentino, to name a few) were then still alive and kicking, but it was true that I was the only student there who wrote stories that looked odd on the page.

"A Story Set in Germany" starts with a warning to readers that this is not an easy story to tell. Then the story is told twice, the first time in a sprightly, fairy-tale voice.

> As a small train steams its way into the mountains an American girl on board is awed and struck by the dense German forests, by the dense German snow. She is going to

live in a farmhouse high above the tiny town called the wild place, *Wildflecken*. Our American girl has a job teaching remedial English to the American soldiers at the post on the mountain opposite the mountain she will come to think of as her mountain, *Ziegelhütte*. The post plays no part in this story; pay no attention to it.

Then the story is told again, this time in a way that reveals the more painful truth. The sections in the second telling are headed with quotations from the original version.

"Our American girl feels right at home because her mother was German."

My mother was a German war bride, but by the time I was born she was an American citizen. German was never spoken in our house unless my mother whispered it to me when I was asleep and safe from its charm. . . .

Once in the house of a grade school best friend I saw a picture over the sofa, a family portrait that had been folded into a dozen tiny squares, then unfolded and framed. Her family, my friend's mother explained to me. All of them died in the concentration camps during the war and only she escaped, carrying that picture folded in her shoe. I understood. My mother had pictures, too, of stiff-collared uncles and brothers and father, and high-haired dark-eyed aunts and sisters and mother. Hers all dead too, in the army, in the bombing, eating sugar beets in the rubble left after the war, but my mother's pictures were not framed on the wall but hidden in her underwear drawer beneath her heavy stitched bras. Because it wasn't the same thing, it wasn't at all.

I told the story this way because I wanted a structure that reflected how hard it was to tell, how when we travel we send one version home in postcards and live another. I couldn't tell it in a more traditional way because for me the story was the structure. In this story I felt form successfully followed function, and I still do. Perhaps you, too, have a story from your life (or you have heard or have imagined) that has so far escaped becoming fiction because it didn't fit into a traditional narrative structure. If you turned your back on traditional short story structure, could you invent a structure that would work?

If you need inspiration, know that there are many examples of structural innovation left by brave writers who went before you. Jorge Luis Borges often wrote "ficciones" that pretended to be nonfiction, taking the form of journal entries, encyclopedia articles and scholarly treatises. "Pierre Menard, Author of Don Quixote" is a short story that masquerades as a treatise. The narrator argues that a twentieth-century Frenchman named Pierre Menard actually wrote the great Spanish novel *Don Quixote de la Mancha* without reference to the original. Menard did his job so well that the two *Don Quixote*s, Cervantes' and Menard's, are identical. The narrator points out that knowing this changes everything we think about the work.

> To compose *Don Quixote* at the beginning of the seven-
> teenth century was a reasonable, necessary and perhaps inevi-
> table undertaking; at the beginning of the twentieth century
> it is almost impossible.

The narrator believes Menard's *Quixote* is superior precisely because, like most experimental work, it is such a difficult or even mad undertaking. Borges is making a serious point: Our knowledge of who a writer was does influence our opinion of his work. At the same time, he is poking fun at both literary scholarship and at his own chosen genre, experimental fiction.

Nicholson Baker's novel *The Mezzanine*, which I used as an example earlier, is another case of fiction borrowing some of its structure from nonfiction. His narrator could not tell his story without the copious footnotes that at first look very odd in a work of fiction. In the text the narrator takes the time to explore why his foot has slipped out of his shoe while he worked at his desk. Then the footnote takes us, appropriately enough, even deeper into the minutiae of his foot theories.

> . . . When you slide a socked foot over a carpeted surface . . .
> though you think you are enjoying the texture of the car-
> peting, you are really enjoying the slippage of the inner sur-
> face of the sock against the underside of your foot, something
> you normally get to experience only in the morning when you
> first pull the sock on.[1]

[1] When I pull a sock on, I no longer *pre-bunch*, that is, I don't gather the sock up into telescoped folds over my thumbs and then position the resultant donut over my toes, even though I believed for some years that this was a clever trick, taught by admirable, fresh-faced kindergarten teachers, and that I revealed my laziness and my inability to plan ahead by instead holding the sock by the ankle rim and jamming my foot to its destination, working the ankle a few times to properly seat the heel.

There is nothing that can't go into a story or novel. I've read fiction making good use of such found forms as singles ads, newspaper articles, self-help books, and daily horoscopes. Is there a nonfiction form that interests you enough to use as the basis for a piece of experimental fiction? At least partly? Think of your fiction as an accordion folder with room for all kinds of odd bits. Sections of Irish writer Samuel Beckett's novel *Watt* include whole songs, musical notation and all. French Surrealist André Breton's novel *Nadja* includes drawings and photographs of people and found objects.

This impulse to perform large-scale, structural experiments has deep roots. Eighteenth-century English writer Laurence Sterne's *Tristram Shandy*, a novel written when the form was still young, is one of the most experimental novels ever written. It purports to be a picaresque novel like Henry Fielding's *Tom Jones*, one that will tell us the story of the birth, childhood, youthful misadventures, and eventual coming into respectable manhood of the eponymous central character. But Sterne's real interest is in making fun of this traditional, slightly stodgy narrative structure. Tristram Shandy begins his story before his birth. Just at the crucial moment he was to be conceived, his mother distracts his father.

> *Pray, my dear,* quoth my mother, have you not forgot to wind up the clock?———Good G—! cried my father, making an exclamation, but taking care to moderate his voice at the same time,———*Did ever woman, since the creation of the world, interrupt a man with such a silly question?*

It is Tristram's theory, developed at great length in the course of the novel, that this distraction influenced the force of both his conception and his personality, leading him to be prone to distraction and digression himself. And he proves it to us, in the course of this long novel, as digression leads to more digression, leaving the story of his life largely untold. Tristram finds room, though, for almost everything else. (Remember, fiction is an ever-expandable accordion folder.) One chapter ends with two pages printed perfectly black, and in another chapter the narrator asks us to draw our own sketch of a character.

> Sit down, Sir, paint her to your own mind————as like your mistress as you can————as unlike your wife as your conscience will let you————'tis all the one to me————please but your own fancy in it.

And then gives us the blank page to do it.

Is there a story or chapter of yours that cries out for illustration? Perhaps for an actual mirror to demonstrate to readers that they are characters too? If Sterne writing in 1759 could turn the still young idea of the novel inside out, there is no idea you could have that is too wild to try.

EXPERIMENTAL LANGUAGE

Fiction, no matter what its architecture, is built with words. Sometimes experimentation takes place not at the larger structural level, but at the basic peg, nail, or screw level. Many twentieth-century experimental writers listened to the words of the people around them, explored their own thoughts, and decided that the conventions of traditional narrative did not reflect reality. Then they set out to find a way to use words to tell what they saw as the truth. Perhaps you have often felt the same gap between the world as you see it and conventional narrative. You might be a writer about to start down the same experimental path.

As we saw when we looked at a passage from Virginia Woolf's novel *Mrs. Dalloway*, in our discussion of point of view, Woolf thought long and hard about what really happens inside people's minds and came up with an experimental approach that dips readers into the stream of consciousness. In Woolf's novel *To the Lighthouse*, Lily Briscoe, returning to stay with the Ramsays, is caught in the swirling eddies of her thoughts and can make no forward progress.

> What does it mean then, what can it all mean? Lily Briscoe asked herself, wondering whether, since she had been left alone, it behoved her to go to the kitchen to fetch another cup

of coffee or wait here. What does it mean?—a catchword that was, caught up from some book, fitting her thought loosely, for she could not, this first morning with the Ramsays, contract her feelings, could only make a phrase resound to cover the blankness of her mind until these vapours had shrunk. For really, what did she feel, come back after all these years and Mrs. Ramsay dead? Nothing, nothing—nothing she could express at all.

The language that Samuel Beckett uses in books like *Watt*, *Molloy*, *Malone Dies*, and *The Unnamable* is also designed to make his readers reconsider the very nature of human thought. Often Beckett's characters question every tiny thing in their movements, thoughts, and environment as if these things had great meaning, or as if nothing had any meaning at all. In Beckett's novel *Watt*, the main character falls into just such a spate of worried wondering as he ponders the visit of a blind piano tuner and his son to the house of his master, Mr. Knott.

What distressed Watt in this incident of the Galls father and son, and in subsequent similar incidents, was not so much that he did not know what had happened, for he did not care what had happened, as that nothing had happened, that a thing that was nothing had happened, with the utmost formal distinctness, and that it continued to happen, in his mind, he supposed, though he did not know exactly what that meant, and though it seemed to be outside him, before him, about him, and so on, inexorably to unroll its phases, beginning with the first (the knock that was not a knock) and ending with the last (the door closing that was not a door closing). . . .

Both Woolf and Beckett believe in the nonstop nature of thought. They move fluidly from one thought to the next in run-on sentences, trying to show us how they believe their characters think. Sometimes, though, writers' visions of how language works in thought and in life has more to do with subtraction than addition, and this, too, shows up in their fiction. Susan Sontag uses a loose outline form in "Project for a Trip to China" to lay out her narrator's thoughts.

● III

The conception of this trip is very old.

First conceived when? As far back as I can remember.
          —Investigate possibility that I was conceived
          in China though born in New York and
          brought up elsewhere (America).
          —write M.
              —telephone?

Here Sontag takes the outline form we use to organize our thoughts for essays to show us how disorganized thoughts really are. If you'll permit me, I'll redo this passage in a Woolf-like stream-of-consciousness style.

> The conception of this trip was very old, she thought, thinking again, again, always again about China, but first conceived when? As far back as she could remember, maybe she had even been born there, before her family moved to New York, to Texas and then, where was it? Oh yes, Arizona. She would have to write her mother, surely she would know. Or should she telephone?

What do you believe people's thoughts are like? Like Hemingway's characters, concise and to the point? Like Woolf's, Beckett's, Sontag's? If you had never seen thoughts written down, how would you capture your own on paper? What words are there right now inside your head? Close your eyes and listen to your mind clicking along. If you go to life for your inspiration, not to other fiction, you may find yourself breaking new ground.

TO EACH HIS OWN

When you write experimental fiction, when you build a story that departs noticeably from the fictional norm, be prepared. You are going to lose readers. Some will look at a novel with footnotes or a short story with a stream-of-consciousness voice and turn away as emphatically as they would from a good buy on an octagonal house. But not all readers. The good news is that the ones who are adventurous and open to experiment may be the very best readers of all. To understand experimentation in fiction for what it is requires a certain level of understanding of fictional structures. These readers understand the nature of the traditional conflict-based plot well enough so that when it is played with, delayed, numbered, sliced, or diced, they can see through the tricks, solving the puzzle and reconstructing the story into a traditional narrative in their own heads. Their reward for the effort is a greater sense of participation.

The more difficult the puzzle, the harder you are asking readers to work and the smaller the number of readers you'll find up to the task. Gertrude Stein built experimental prose word by word, structural element by element. She may have pushed language farther toward abstraction than any other writer of our time, and that is saying a good deal. Not incidentally some of her most experimental stories and novels go virtually unread today, and the most widely read, *Three Lives*, a set of interconnected stories, is an early and much less experimental work.

Being an experimental writer is a quest that may take you farther and farther into a world of your own creation and away from one most others would willingly occupy. The nineteenth-century English explorer, translator, and writer Sir Richard Burton traveled the world almost unceasingly, learning languages wherever he went. His first accounts of his travels, such as his journey to Mecca and Medina, were widely read. By the time his later books were published, he had developed a system of references so complicated that few but Sir Richard Burton himself could follow them. His account of a journey to Iceland carries this to such an extreme, describing every rock and every custom by comparing it to another found in some even more obscure corner of the world, that it is virtually unreadable except perhaps by someone who has read all of Burton's work with extreme care. Fictional worlds can become equally daunting to readers.

I tell you this not to scare you back onto the straight and narrow path, narratively speaking, but so you cannot later say I didn't warn you. If you are an explorer by nature, a mere well-intended warning will not stop you. It certainly wouldn't have stopped the great Irish writer James Joyce. When he published his early short-story collection *Dubliners* in 1914, it was viewed as experimental in both its content and technique, but few readers would have difficulty with it now. The use of dashes instead of quotation marks to set off dialogue still looks a bit unusual on the page, but this conversation from "Araby" between the narrator, his aunt, and his uncle is fairly easy to follow.

> I did not smile. My aunt said to him energetically:
> —Can't you give him the money and let him go? You've kept him late enough as it is.
> My uncle said he was very sorry he had forgotten. He said he believed in the old saying: *All work and no play makes Jack a dull boy.* He asked me where I was going. . . .

But Joyce was just starting on his quest, his grand experiment with structure and language. His 1922 novel, *Ulysses*, made him famous. This work of genius starts with conversations between the central character, Stephen Dedalus, and his friends written in much the same form as the section of "Araby" I quoted above. By the end the book has reached a different plane. It is hard to think of fiction and what it can do in quite the same way after reading Molly Bloom's famous soliloquy. The book ends with her voice.

> the night we missed the boat at Algeciras the watchman going about serene with his lamp and O that awful deepdown torrent O and the sea the sea crimson sometimes like fire and the glorious sunsets and the figtrees in the Alameda gardens and all the queer little streets and pink and blue and yellow houses and the rosegardens and the jessamine and geraniums and cactuses and Gibraltar as a girl where I was a Flower of the mountain yes when I put the rose in my hair like the Andalusian girls used or shall I wear a red yes and how he kissed me under the Moorish wall and I thought well as well him as another and then I asked him with my eyes to ask again yes and then he asked me would I yes to say yes my mountain flower and first I put my arms around him yes and drew him down to me so he could feel my breasts all perfume yes and his heart was going like mad and yes I said yes I will Yes.

Joyce didn't stop there, nor do I mean to imply he should have. His fiction kept evolving. Still, reading the opening of his last novel, *Finnegans Wake*, makes it clear why it is famous for being one of those books more talked about than read.

riverrun, past Eve and Adam's, from swerve of shore to bend of bay, brings us by a commodius vicus of recirculation back to Howth Castle and Environs.

Sir Tristram, violer d'amores, fr'over the short sea, had passencore rearrived from North Amorica on this side the scraggy isthmus of Europe Minor to wielderfight his penisolate war; nor had topsawyer's rocks by the stream Oconee exaggerated themselse to Laurens County's gorgios while they went doublin their mumper all the time; nor avoice from afire bellowsed mishe mishe to tauftauf thuartpeatrick . . .

Like the Middle English of Chaucer's *Canterbury Tales*, *Finnegans Wake* benefits from being read aloud, when the odd spellings quit troubling the eye so much and the flow of the language takes over. I once went to a performance that consisted of everyone being given a few pages torn from a paperback copy of *Finnegans Wake*. We were all asked to read our pages out loud at the same time in the courtyard of the art museum that was hosting the event. Not the perfect way to absorb the whole work, but all of us got very caught up in our part of it. Twenty minutes later when it was over, several artists and even an innocent passerby or two swore the event had convinced them to read the whole book. I hope some of them did, and I urge you, brave writer, to do likewise. Or to read or reread *Ulysses*. By the end Joyce's language will seem natural to you. Then you can sit down and stretch your own linguistic boundaries.

EXERCISES

1. Sit quietly and listen to your thoughts. Let your thoughts go where they will, and gently note their direction. Now try to recreate them in writing. Like writing down a dream, just the act of recording your thoughts changes their nature, but do the best you can.

2. Now take a fictional character, yours or someone else's, and try to transcribe his thoughts the same way. Read what you've written when you're finished. What does it teach you about how thoughts work? If you can, use part of what you've written about yourself or your character in a short story or novel.

3. Go into a room where no one can hear you and start talking. Either transcribe what you are saying (if you are a fast typist or have

good handwriting) or use a tape recorder and transcribe it later. Just talk about your life or your history or what you like to eat. Let one thing lead naturally to another.

4. Now do the same thing for a character from your own or someone else's fiction. Either lend the character your voice and talk out loud or do it silently by letting the voice fill your head. Either way, write down a monologue. When you're done look over what you've written. Is it different than the dialogue you usually see in stories or the dialogue you write yourself? How? What does it teach you about the spoken narrative voice? If you can, use part of what you've written in a short story or novel.

5. Find a written form that exists in the world outside fiction (a letter, an ad, an encyclopedia article, a cookbook), and use it in some way in a story or novel. It can shape the entire piece the way the idea of the scholarly article shapes Borges' "Pierre Menard, Author of Don Quixote," or it can merely appear, the way the song lyrics do in Beckett's novel *Watt*.

6. It helps to have a large table or patch of clear floor for this exercise. Take a story you have written or a photocopy of a published story you've read and cut it up so each paragraph or scene is on a separate slip of paper. Rearrange the slips so the ending comes first and the other pieces are randomly scrambled. Now read the story. Can you decode the puzzle and figure out what the story is about? Shift some of the slips around until it works better, but no fair putting it back as it was. The goal is to find a form you actually like better than the original.

7. Find at least two rules or bits of good advice I have given you in this book and write a wonderful piece of fiction that successfully breaks both.

ABOUT THE AUTHOR

Jesse Lee Kercheval was born in France and raised in Florida. She is the author of the story collection *The Dogeater*, which won the Associated Writing Programs Award for Short Fiction, and a novel, *The Museum of Happiness*. Her memoir, *Space*, is being published by Algonquin in fall 1997. Her fiction and poetry appear regularly in magazines in the United States, England, Japan, and Australia and have won her awards from the National Endowment for the Arts, the Bunting Institute, James A. Michener, and the Wisconsin Arts Board. She teaches creative writing at the University of Wisconsin in Madison.

INDEX

More From Story Press

Revision: A Creative Approach to Writing and Rewriting Fiction, by David Michael Kaplan. Join David Kaplan as he demonstrates how creative the revision process can be through every stage of story-writing, providing strategies and criteria to help you pinpoint and fix problems in your work. Plus, he offers a rare and personal look at revision by showing how three of his own short stories evolved. *#48024/$18.99/240 pages*

Elements of the Writing Craft, by Robert Olmstead. Never before have the elements of writing—and the process of reading like a writer—been presented in such an intelligent and accessible format. In this landmark book, Robert Olmstead reveals how noted writers have "built" their fiction and nonfiction. There are over 150 lessons and each contains a short passage from a distinguished writer, a writer's-eye analysis of the passage, and innovative writing exercises to help you apply the techniques of the masters in your own work. *#48027/$19.99/272 pages*

The Joy of Writing Sex, by Elizabeth Benedict. Finally, here's the book to help you craft intimate scenes that are original, sensitive and just right for your fiction. Elizabeth Benedict's instruction, supported with examples from the finest contemporary fiction, focuses on creating sensual encounters that hinge on freshness of character, dialogue, mood and plot. You'll also find spirited opinions from some of today's most prestigious writers—among them, John Updike, Dorothy Allison, Russell Banks and Joyce Carol Oates. *#48021/$16.99/160 pages*

The ABC's of Writing Fiction, by Ann Copeland. With a teaching style that's dynamic and offbeat, Ann Copeland offers an authoritative wealth of instruction, advice and insight on the writing life. Penetrating alphabetical mini-lessons and unexpected words and phrases—culled from 15 years of teaching fiction—encourage browsing, free associating and random discoveries. *#48017/$18.99/256 pages*

Turning Life Into Fiction, by Robin Hemley. Writers' lives, those of their friends and family members, newspaper accounts, conversations overheard—these can be the bases for novels and short stories. Here, Robin Hemley shows how to make true stories even better. You'll learn how to turn journal entries into fiction; find good story material within yourself; identify memories that can be developed; and fictionalize other people's stories. Exercises guide writers in honing their skills. *#48000/$17.99/208 pages*

Fiction Writer's Workshop, by Josip Novakovich. In this interactive workshop, you'll explore each aspect of the art of fiction including point of view, description, revision, voice and more. At the end of each chapter you'll find more than a dozen writing exercises to help you put what you've learned into action. *#48003/$17.99/256 pages*

The Fiction Dictionary, by Laurie Henry. The essential guide to the inside language of fiction. These are terms from yesterday, today—and even those just being coined for the language of tomorrow. Some you've heard of; others may open up exciting new possibilities in your own writing. You'll discover genres you've never explored, writing devices you'll want to attempt, fresh characters to populate your stories. *The Fiction Dictionary* dusts off the traditional concept of "dictionary" by giving full, vivid descriptions, and by using lively examples from classic and contemporary fiction . . . turning an authoritative reference into a can't-put-it-down browser. *#48008/$18.99/336 pages*

Idea Catcher, from the Editors of Story Press. This spirited journal will help you open your eyes to the creative possibilities in your everyday world. You'll find something on every page of this journal to stimulate your senses and spark your imagination. *Idea Catcher* will teach you to use rich, surprising sources of inspiration through several writing "prompts." Plus, you'll find insightful quotes from well-known writers and short anecdotes about how authors "caught" the ideas that became great works of literature. *#48011/$14.99/160 pages*